y

Scrubbed Out

Reviving the Doctor's Role in Patient Care

Salah D. Salman M.D.

authorHOUSE®

AuthorHouse™
1663 Liberty Drive
Bloomington, IN 47403
www.authorhouse.com
Phone: 1-800-839-8640

First published by AuthorHouse 9/29/2011

ISBN: 978-1-4634-2820-4 (e)
ISBN: 978-1-4634-2818-1 (hc)
ISBN: 978-1-4634-2819-8 (sc)

Library of Congress Control Number: 2011910326

Printed in the United States of America

Dedication

This book is dedicated to the colleagues, trainees, and students who, knowingly or unknowingly, generously supplied me with material for its critical content, and to the others who were too busy, too indifferent, or too scared to speak their minds or even publically comment on important issues in health care. May this book help their sense of responsibility grow and develop.

It is also dedicated to the new breed of leaders in medicine, waiting to be identified, who are needed to design, execute, and monitor the unavoidable health care reform.

Table of Contents

Preface

When I left Lebanon and immigrated to the U.S. in 1986, I was fatigued and drained by eleven years of civil war and by my public service as the Lebanese minister of the interior. I was eager to resume my career in academic medicine as an ear, nose, and throat specialist in a better environment. I was privileged and lucky to be offered positions at two world-famous and leading medical institutions, the Massachusetts Eye and Ear Infirmary (MEEI) and Harvard Medical School. Two major aims in my life had been to teach and to try to make a difference in my community and my profession. I thought Boston, the medical capital of the world, would provide me with a golden opportunity to better serve these aims and to try to influence a larger circle than that available to me in Beirut.

Throughout my twenty-three-year career in Boston, I had the pleasure to meet and interact with masters in my field and with groups of smart, motivated students and residents. But a part of my experience was surprising and not rewarding at all: I made observations in the leading institutions at which I worked in particular, and in the American health care system in general, that deeply appalled me. As I witnessed repeated failings, I started early on keeping a record of significant occurrences and experiences. The large number of health care problems, deficiencies, and errors I observed at MEEI, Massachusetts General Hospital (MGH), and Harvard Medical School over twenty-three years are the subject of this book. I tell stories and present reflections as a full-time, hospital-based doctor, as a teacher, and as a patient myself. This book is very much a personal viewpoint, not a study or a survey of the American health care system, the hospitals, or the medical profession.

This book is unique in that it presents the perspectives of one caring medical doctor, which are different from those adopted by the major health decision makers, who have successfully excluded the medical profession almost entirely during decision making and while seeking an expected timely reform. It is not my aim to criticize political ideologies and economic theories. I aim to shed light on shady practices of the major health decision makers and hospitals that write the rules, regulations, and laws that govern the practice, research, and teaching of medicine. These have contributed significantly to the present crisis and have stood in the way of effective reform. The book directs the spotlight on ignored, ugly corners of the health care landscape. It is also unique in that it does not shy away from finger-pointing if necessary, and from publically criticizing colleagues, major teaching institutions, and professional societies, heretofore a taboo among doctors.

This book does more than criticize, however; it provides unorthodox, "politically incorrect" solutions that are necessary for reform but that are largely impossible to implement and even voice in the current political climate and available venues. I hope that the solutions proposed in this book will serve as a nucleus for timely, radical reform, or even a revolution, if it proves unavoidable. This book's tone is urgent; I am concerned that the current cost-cutting measures that are to be adopted in the reform process by corporations and hospitals will not serve the patients and the public health well, and will not work adequately in the long run.

I am unabashedly idealistic in proposing solutions, but I am not a naïve, unrealistic dreamer. I am convinced that when a job needs to be done, leaders should do it. My experience as a professor and chairman of an academic department in the Faculty of Medicine at the American University of Beirut taught me that it is possible for a leader in a teaching institution to make a *big* difference in health care, if the intent is present. Likewise, my experience as a minister of the interior in the Lebanese cabinet taught me that there is always at least *something* that can be done to improve very complex situations, even during civil wars. The other option for leaders would be to sit back, witness situations evolve and deteriorate, and then claim that efforts for improvement are futile. Unfortunately, current medical leaders have opted for the latter option. In contrast, I believe that health care is a nonnegotiable human right, that the practice of medicine is a mission more than a business, and that doctors have an unwritten contract with society to provide health services. I believe that health care is the ultimate responsibility of the medical profession, and nobody else's. Doctors carry a double responsibility to society, first as citizens, and second as the major guardians of health.

In order to explain how I have arrived at my convictions, I should explain my background. I was raised in a Lebanese family and am one of six children. Both of my parents have influenced my career through exemplary behavior and ideals. My parents believed in and practiced philanthropy. They were in part motivated by the ideals of our religion, Druze, which is a small Unitarian sect that stemmed from Islam in the eleventh century AD. My father, a general medical doctor, graduated in 1922 from the American University of Beirut, which was founded in 1866 by American missionaries. He was taught that medicine was a calling and a mission, a science and an art in the service of the sick. He saw patients for free two half-days a week. My mother was a college graduate, an uncommon occurrence then among women of conservative Druze families. Besides raising six children, she consecrated her life to working for the welfare of children as a volunteer and leader. She was often referred to in the media and in public meetings as the mother of all Lebanese children.

My parents' examples inspired me to study medicine. As an undergraduate at the American University of Beirut, I obtained an excellent education that further reinforced my ideals. Teachers of medicine then behaved like role models. During my education and thereafter, I was privileged to have had many leadership and service opportunities that helped shape my mind and attitudes and allowed me to formulate a blueprint for my life's dreams. I became convinced that leaders in any field can make a difference if they choose to; otherwise they do not belong in leadership positions.

It is because of my convictions and my personal experiences as a leader that I have been so disappointed by the leadership in the U.S. medical system, not only in its failure to fulfill its unwritten contract with society to provide adequate health care, but also in its relative indifference to forces and pressures that contaminated the practice of medicine and rendered it a business.

That said, to criticize one's profession is no simple or casual undertaking. It took a great deal of soul-searching for me to decide to write this book. As ideas crystallized in my mind, I sought the opinion of friends, who all exhibited the same initial reaction: "Are you crazy? Are you aware of all the risks you are taking?" They made a good point; by daring to say the unspeakable, criticizing, and questioning the judgment and motivations of the powerful demigods of Boston medicine, I risked making enemies among colleagues, hospitals, and universities, and even losing my job.

My friends were perhaps wise to caution me. But in the end, my loyalty to my profession in particular and to society in general proved stronger than my loyalty to my employers, my university, and to certain famous colleagues and friends who do not all deserve their fame. Also, the fact that I decided to retire facilitated my eventual decision to go ahead with my book project.

While I continue to be proud of my years of association with two giant Boston medical institutions and am indeed grateful for the horizons they allowed me to explore and for the opportunities they provided me, gratefulness is not a good enough reason to muzzle myself. Besides, keeping quiet in the face of serious problems is not a healthy manifestation of, or requirement for, loyalty. Indeed, I consider the silent "see no evil" attitude, widely practiced by the medical profession, responsible for many of the problems in health care.

Is it quixotic to hope that, by speaking up and openly criticizing the medical profession and leading teaching institutions, I and other caring medical professionals can make a difference? Is it futile to propose a different health care system that is better than the present one? Is it overly idealistic to try to extricate health care from the legal and commercial forces that continue to complicate it and even suffocate it? Is it impossible to rehabilitate medical doctors and remake them into professional healers, like their predecessors, rather than health care "deliverers" and businessmen in a health care industry controlled by corporations and a corporate mentality? Is it impossible to free health care from the dominating, not-always-positive influence of the insurance and the pharmaceutical companies? Is the imposing and costly presence of bureaucrats, administrators, and lawyers a necessity? Is it useless and futile to ask the medical profession to police itself for quality and cost-control in a traditional, time-tested manner? Is it unreasonable to expect medical leaders to lead in a responsible direction, rather than succumb to the external pressures and forces that contributed to or caused the health care problems? With tens of millions of uninsured and underinsured citizens, in the strongest world economy, is it utopian to hope that the federal and various state legislatures can ever be motivated to introduce and impose universal health care, like it has been for years in other, less affluent, industrialized countries?

Is it unreasonable to expect the medical profession to reassume its traditional and natural role of patients' advocacy, and fight and refuse to comply with unnecessary costly rules and regulations that do not make sense and that have not achieved their intended purposes?

My answer to all these questions is an emphatic *no*. This book is a signal that I have not given up, in spite of the advice volunteered by friends, who asked me to be pragmatic and "a man of this world." The missionary spark that I acquired, first at home and later in medical school and after personal experiences, is still active and refuses to die. Defeatism should not masquerade as realism; we, as medical professionals and citizens, have a duty to speak our minds and to fight for fairness, justice, and equality. Accordingly, I have opted to act responsibly, and exercise candidly the vanishing right of free speech. I admit without apologies that, in the process, shedding the common and popular political correctness proved necessary.

Acknowledgments

The author would like to thank Jack Satter, Jane T. Fogg, and Farida Al-Zamil for their generous support of this book project.

Chapter One
Health Care Is a Neglected Human Right in the United States

The Need for a New Health Care System

"Insurers cheat the patients and doctors, patients cheat doctors and insurers, doctors cheat insurers and patients, and all cheat federal and state governments."

Barlett and Steele

Universal Health Care

These days, it is pretty rare for liberals and conservatives to see eye to eye on anything, but one thing is clear: no one is happy with health care in the United States except corporations. While not everybody agrees on the best way to enact health care reform, there seems to be unanimous agreement about its necessity; however, the acclaimed 2010 health care bill has not guaranteed the needed universal health care. Negotiations to remedy problems within the system rarely involve all the parties concerned; notably absent is the medical profession, which has been systematically marginalized. Cooperative efforts to solve health care problems have not been seriously initiated, even in the present crisis. The insurance companies, the current major players, and decision makers are fixated on the bottom line and stand in the way of needed reform. The transformation of the practice of medicine into a business for providing health care has been a strong blow to the time-honored traditional practice of medicine, and has disrupted the all-important patient-doctor relationship.

The United States needs a universal health care system, which is already

1

available in less affluent industrialized countries. I believe that health care is a human right, and it has been neglected in this country. Other essential services are provided by the government—why not health care? Everyone is guaranteed a free elementary and high school education in the public school systems, and security, personal and national, is available to all. The logical solution to our health care problem is a single-payer system, run by the government or a government agency. Our capitalist infrastructure has prevented the creation of such a system up until this point, mainly because our original health care system was built around private, rather than public, insurance companies.

Many involved parties have stood in the way of the needed reform, including prominent medical associations and societies. Why has the medical profession, well versed in the principles of prevention, not exercised its expertise in recent decades to prevent serious health care problems? The idea of prevention is as old as medicine. Lessons about how to avoid common colds during the winter months have been passed down from family to family for centuries. Patients with infectious diseases, like measles, should be isolated to prevent the spread of the disease to those around them. The sterile technique has made major contributions in the development of safer surgeries: all operating personnel wear sterile gowns and gloves after scrubbing or disinfecting hands and forearms, and the operative sites are sterilized whenever possible. Certain body areas are impossible to sterilize, like the mouth and nose, but the sterile technique protects against the introduction of new bacteria during the operation, as much as possible. The preventive immunizations have mostly, or completely, eradicated many serious diseases, like smallpox and polio, and with successful methods of fighting mosquitoes, malaria has become a less serious world problem. With the aim of preventing more serious problems, tough decisions sometimes have to be made. For centuries, legs have been amputated—because of diabetic, gangrenous toes or severe war injuries—in order to avoid more serious complications or even death. Those working in the health care field have allowed some health problems to persist or go from bad to worse without serious interference or responsible, corrective action. Hospital-acquired infections and medication errors continue to occur. Recurring serious problems continue to increase in number and seriousness. The estimated up to ninety-eight thousand deaths per year that result from medical errors, according to one Institute of Medicine study, illustrate this point very clearly.[1]

---

1   Institute of Medicine, *To Err Is Human, Building a Safer Health System* (Washington DC: National Academy Press, 2000), 26.

Most parties involved in or affected by the health care system—patients, hospital administrators, doctors, and nurses—are not happy with the current system, the cost of which continues to escalate. There seems to be a general feeling of futility among doctors and nurses when it comes to expressing dissatisfaction and proposing solutions. Few serious efforts to intervene in the system have been mobilized (a counterexample is the nationwide campaign to ensure hand washing in clinics and hospitals), since medical professionals assume they are helpless to influence health care. All too often, patients and doctors accept what they experience and observe, and don't bother to do anything about it.

Polls that are currently reported in the media consistently show that the majority of voters support a public option in addition to private insurers, in order to provide the sought-after universal health care system. The current national health care plan for seniors (Medicare) is successful and popular, so why not adopt something similar for those who choose it? The country is not ready yet for a single-payer system, like a government-run universal care system. However, Congress does not want to displace the powerful private insurance industry of our capitalist system with a government-run, national health insurance system. Politicians receive significant contributions from wealthy private insurance companies; in return, they tend to vote with their funders' interests in mind. The arguments they voice are not always in the interest of patients. The government "of the people, by the people, and for the people" has failed in health care to deserve its appellation. The federal government continues to be more responsive to corporate needs than to public health. However, with the problems and decline of the health care system, the government will have to adopt a universal plan sooner or later. Until very recently, health care reform was not given priority in Congress, because the public in general and the uninsured in general have not capitalized on their potential power and have failed to put enough pressure on legislators. Up until the 2008 presidential election, health care was never made a priority—except rhetorically—during election campaigns. Since President Obama pledged to fix it, it has finally become a hot issue and a realizable aim, unless conservatives succeed in preventing him.

The current health care system leaves a lot to be desired and needs to be reformed, as the current health landscape clearly demonstrates. The insurance premiums continue to rise, and 15 percent of the population (46 million) had no health insurance coverage in 2007. In 1980, the numbers were 8 percent (26.6 million). Seniors are alarmed because they may not be able to pay out of pocket for all of their prescription medications. There are disparities in the quality of health care received in the United States that are dependent on ethnicity, socioeconomic status, geography, and doctors' availability. Over the years, the health status of Americans has continued to drop, and the costs have kept increasing. Our infant mortality and low-birth-weight rates have not dropped over the years. More than 40 percent of the population is taking at least one prescription drug, and one out of every six Americans takes three or more prescription drugs. The prevalence of obesity in people aged twenty to seventy-four has increased in the last two decades from 47 percent to 65 percent. Meanwhile, between 1980 and 2002, the yearly per capita health care spending increased by 410 percent, from $1,067 to $5,414. [2]Drug expenditures by patients were $12 billion in 1980. By 2002, the figure climbed to $162 billion, a 1,250 percent increase.[3]

Newer, more expensive medications are flooding the market, and patients pressure doctors to prescribe them even when there is no proof that they are superior to older and less expensive ones. Insurers are unhappy with surgeons who over-operate and with physicians who overprescribe new and expensive medications, especially antibiotics. Doctors' incomes are decreasing, while their expenses keep growing, and as a result some seek to increase their productivity and income at the expense of quality, although this fact is never openly admitted. The popular practice of defensive medicine is costly and not always justifiable. The risk of costly, lengthy, and very unpleasant malpractice lawsuits—whether frivolous or justified—is always on doctors' minds, so they tend to over-order expensive tests, over-refer to consultants, and overprescribe expensive new medications that are aggressively advertised. This defensive practice is to make sure they are not liable if they are late suspecting an unlikely diagnosis, no matter how unlikely it is. Not every patient with a headache needs an MRI to rule out a brain tumor. As a result, malpractice insurance rates go up, further raising costs. Some specialists pay over one hundred thousand dollars per year to their malpractice insurers.

Meanwhile, the shortage of nurses has reached an alarming level, and has not been seriously addressed. Hospitals are struggling to survive—or so claim their highly paid administrators. Yet they continue to grow. For

2   Donald L. Barlett and James B. Steele, *Critical Condition: How Health Care in America Became Big Business and Bad Medicine* (New York: Doubleday, 2004), 24.

3   Barlett and Steele, *Critical Condition*, 35.

example, since 1986, when I arrived in Boston, I have witnessed never-ending building activities at the Massachusetts General Hospital and the Massachusetts Eye and Ear Infirmary where I worked.

National education and security are taken for granted as human rights, but why do we have to lobby and fight, so far unsuccessfully, for basic universal health care, another human right?

To cover the increasing costs, insurance companies increase their rates and reduce benefits whenever they want to. Medicare costs were 256.8 billion in 2002, 440 billion in 2007, and reached 559 billion in 2008.[4]

Where is all of this money going? Western countries with less money, like the U.K., France, and Canada, offer health care to all their citizens. Why can't we do the same? Among thirty-three industrialized countries, the U.S. is tied with Hungary, Malta, Poland, and Slovakia with an infant death rate of 5/1000[5].

The excuses decision makers provide are not sufficient to justify a sad status quo. In Canada, we are reminded that patients cannot always pick their doctor, and they have to wait lengthy periods for appointments. Therefore, the Canadian system is not good enough for the U.S., claim those who oppose a serious reform. Don't we suffer currently from the same issues?

Much of health care is controlled by third parties, mostly the government, the employers, the pharmaceutical industry, and the insurers—rather than those most directly affected and involved. Doctors and nurses are missing in boardrooms and in debates, and patients have no committed advocates. Insurance companies, bureaucrats, and administrators have a field day making unilateral decisions that suit them, even if they do not serve public health. Corporations and market forces, rather than patients and doctors, hold the greatest sway over health care and make the decisions that most directly impact health. They have the power to impose their choices and are not held accountable for the outcomes of their decisions. Serious, and often suppressed, questions remain: why have these third parties been permitted to hold so much power, and why have they gotten away with decisions that do not serve the public's health?

Medical doctors, health insurers, and hospital administrators have gradually developed independent work practices; they have little concern

---

4   http://sweetness-light.com/archives/none-noted-medicaid-at-medicare-signing

5   Lindsey Tanner, "U.S. Scores Poorly on Infant Mortality," Associated Press, May 9, 2006.

for the other groups' interests. Each industry has its own agenda to respect, and these agendas are often incompatible with one another. It's not surprising that conflicts of interest continuously develop. The tunnel vision among the different groups, dictated first and foremost by self-interest, needs to end.

Bureaucrats, administrators, lawyers, pharmaceutical companies, and insurance companies have succeeded in establishing themselves as the pillars of the health care decision-making process, and are responsible to a great extent for the intimidation and the increasing marginalization of medical doctors. Gradually, it has become acceptable and even routine for powerful health insurers, administrators, and regulators to impose their decisions on doctors and nurses. The docility of doctors has facilitated this unnecessary, costly, and unwise dominance.

It is common for rules and regulations to be changed on short notice or even retroactively. Pro forma and unconvincing explanations for these changes may or may not be offered.

Doctors ask no questions and raise no objections, yet they are not happy with the continuing loss of their autonomy and the fact that insurers are setting the rules for diagnostic and therapeutic procedures. The marginalization of MDs has led them to become more passive and self-protective. They have lost much of their confidence about their capability to positively influence health care, despite the very basic fact that they are its main pillars. It seems as if they have given up. The rise of materialism, increasing expenses, greedy human nature, and the absence of effective quality and utilization controls have made it easier for doctors to digest and adjust to changes that masquerade as evolution or progress, rather than fight them.

In short, the failing health care system is being overseen by interest groups that distrust one another and vigilantly block rules and laws that may be unfavorable to their interests. I believe that health care professionals should assume control of health care in the United States, to get the system out of the mess that it is currently in. With its traditions and training, a reformed medical profession is the only party that can provide the right health care. I say "reformed," because the current medical profession has failed to scrutinize health care and its leadership, and is partially responsible for today's mess. The health care profession has accepted its marginalization without significant battles, and seems satisfied with making money, rather than fighting for improved care and better resources. It has sold its soul, ignored some of its responsibilities, and underestimated its potential power.

It has picked political correctness over doing the right thing. Medical leaders' dictatorship and their sensitivity to criticisms have had serious negative effects. Doctors and nurses do not bother to criticize and suggest solutions anymore.

Many of the problems and stories this book relates could and should have been prevented by vigilant, caring medical and nursing professions that instead have resigned their responsibilities and allowed health care to be taken over by other parties and influenced by market forces. It is time for medical professionals to step up and assume the responsibilities toward patients for which they have spent years of training.

Thankfully, there is hope that we can turn things around. Despite all of these problems, the medical care available in the United States tends to be excellent, but uneven and expensive. Life expectancy in the United States reached 77.9 years in 2009, the highest it has ever been.[6], and the rates of the three leading causes of death—heart disease, cancer, and stroke—have decreased over the last several decades. Because of America's worldwide reputation, patients, medical students, and visitors come here from all over the world to be treated, to study, or simply to observe. In the twentieth century, there were 183 Nobel laureates in medicine and physiology. Eighty-four of them, 46 percent, were from the United States. In the last third of the century, that figure rose to 62 percent. If doctors step up and take back control of the system, the United States has the potential to excel more in health care.

A Worsening Problem

The current state of health care in America should cause serious concern to all. The system we have now not only affects the present, but also the future quality of medicine in the United States, and even the world. The rise of the corporate mentality, the weakness of traditional quality teaching in medical schools, the diminishment of leadership in the field, and the adoption of strategies concerned first and foremost with balancing budgets and increasing income have all contributed to the alarming present state of health care. The essential humanness of medicine has lost ground. With the advent of the information age and technological advances, medicine has moved closer to becoming a cold science and further from being the

---

6   Reuters, "U.S. life expectancy hits a new high of 78," *Reuters.com*, August 19, 2009, http://www.reuters.com/article/2009/08/20/us-usa-lifespan-idUSTRE5716BF20090820.

caring and warm art it is also supposed to be. It has become more about treating symptoms than caring for patients. For uncontested reasons of "pragmatism" and "the reality of the situation," care, an essential element of medicine, is vanishing.

Other persistent problems contaminate the landscape further. Doctors cheat the system at every step of the way, imitating the practices of insurers and administrators. It should be no surprise that some doctors, to protect their interests, look for ways to get around unfair and unpopular regulations—and they certainly can and often do succeed. For example, medication samples that are not supposed to be in hospital doctors' offices are routinely handed to patients, rather than going through hospital pharmacies as the user-unfriendly regulations require. Irresponsible practices and efforts to outsmart or bypass the system have grown as doctors attempt to recuperate financial losses and cover the increasing expenses forced upon them. Because of their frustration and inability to make changes or even influence decision makers, they have developed new, self-centered attitudes. Over the years, I have witnessed malpractice, mistakes, and substandard care that go unreported or unnoticed. There is an absence of effective self-policing—except on paper. The genuine fear of malpractice lawsuits has not proven to be an effective quality-control motivation. Medical doctors are guilty of not trying to correct errors they witness, and are unable to stop or divert unwise and dangerous trends; they have unfortunately opted for silence rather than responsible behavior. The code of ethics of the AMA requires doctors to report mistakes, but does not specify to whom to report. The medical profession has failed dismally in its quality-control efforts and in rehabilitating or getting rid of the bad lemons in the profession. As a result, doctors have lost a lot of public support and the privileged status they used to enjoy. Instead, they have developed a growing reputation of greed—a reputation not always deserved or justified.

The practice of medicine has become a business of delivering health care, and medical doctors have become businessmen. As a result, doctors unavoidably devote more time and effort to lucrative practices and ignore the less lucrative parts of their practice. Contact time with patients has dropped significantly so doctors may see more patients. Surgical solutions to health problems have become more popular among surgeons than conservative solutions. I have witnessed doctors' biases for more lucrative operations firsthand; surgeries for back pain and sinus headaches are two common examples.

Hospitals attract more public sympathy than doctors, mainly because of clever public relations and marketing campaigns that, even during these hard days, seem to have no funding obstacles. Such campaigns do not always tell the whole truth, and some of their "facts" can't be checked.

Hospitals dodge public outcry when they mercilessly ignore issues necessary for quality care, like sufficient nursing and emergency-room staffing. They are easily forgiven for their overbilling "errors." Their doctors, on the other hand, are pilloried for the same conduct. Resorting to PR campaigns, rather than addressing issues directly, succeeds only in creating a palpably obvious whitewash. The appearance of propriety and the creation of comprehensive legal protections to render the hospitals and the insurers bulletproof have become more important than propriety itself.

Organized cheating of the system has slowly crept onto the scene and become tolerated. It seems that all concerned parties have opted for silence rather than the responsible behavior of speaking out. The line between cheating and serving self-interests (so-called smartness) is becoming hazy. Athletes who take anabolic steroids to win games or races, and advertisers who show only data that suits their interests and ignore those that do not, are just two examples of this new reality. Blue Cross Blue Shield of Massachusetts (BCBSMA), the biggest health insurer in the state, claims in its ads that it played an important role in the progressive new law that Massachusetts passed in 2006. It does *not* inform the ad's viewers that, at the same time, it has increased its rates and decreased the benefits of its subscribers.

The IRS reported that taxes owed but not collected in 2001 ranged from $312–$353 billion.[7] Does this figure point to cheating or cleverness on the part of large corporations, or to IRS incompetence in assuming its responsibilities? Accounting firms and law firms are masters of exploiting tax shelters. Likewise, any motivated, objective observer from within the health care system can easily spot how common deception is. Cheating by doctors and other health care personnel is a very serious issue that deserves much more attention than it has been given so far. If the business of medicine tolerates it, the ethics of medicine should not.

Many of these important issues have been chronically ignored or covered up because of the growing, strong union mentality within the health care organizations. Responsible, medicine-based leadership has been gradually replaced by union-type leadership, which tends to focus on rights

---

7   Robert Kuttner, "The Biggest Tax Cheats," *Boston Globe*, April 13, 2005.

and benefits, rather than on responsible behavior and the mission of the profession; leaders have also adopted a corporate mentality. To make the situation worse, even medical schools and teaching centers have redefined leadership duties. Presidents and deans are recruited for their fundraising potential and administrative skills, not for their leadership, scholarship, or inspirational qualities. This style and type of leadership has to change in the forthcoming health care reform.

In this climate, the healing of patients, the ultimate aim of health care, often becomes secondary and forgotten. Most doctors no longer play the old role of patient advocates; they have resigned this natural responsibility. Patient advocates appointed by hospital administrators, who are actually both the defendants and the jury in cases of complaints, are usually ineffective, and serve merely as window dressing. It is safe to say that currently there are few, if any, serious patient advocates. Though patients are frequently unhappy with the care they receive, they either choose to remain quiet (partially out of fear of legal or financial repercussions, and partially out of fear of not receiving good treatment should they return for care at a later date), or attempt to speak out and are not heard. The objecting voices in our society are neither loud nor persistent enough; they remain unheard in boardrooms and the government.

In general, responsible behavior is desired and universally taught at home, in educational institutions, and in houses of worship. Irresponsible behavior is frowned upon and may even be punishable by law. Yet, as our world is changing, one cannot help but notice that irresponsible behavior in health care seems to be gaining ground and becoming tolerated and even expected. A larger symptom of this problem is the way in which the threat of litigation changes how society at large acts. For example, the desire of a health care professional, or of anybody for that matter, to rush to help a sick or a wounded person on the street is not as strong as it used to be, because of fears of protracted involvement and litigation. It's true that federal and local Good Samaritan laws give general immunity to those who voluntarily assist victims of accidents or crime without compensation or expectation of compensation, yet these laws don't seem to protect adequately against such litigation.

Criticism, dissidence, and debates about important medical or administrative issues are neither encouraged nor tolerated in hospitals (as will be detailed in chapter 4). They are usually treated as unwelcome. When they do happen, political correctness—to save violators and organizations from embarrassment or to keep sensitive issues under cover—dominates the discussions. Usually, no blame or responsibility is assigned, even when blame is entirely appropriate. As a concrete example, every July, incoming residents at the Massachusetts Eye and Ear Infirmary (MEEI) are taught—secretly or implicitly—by older residents not to argue, ask embarrassing questions, or disagree with superiors. Such traditions of silence and docility are very strong among residents nationwide.

It is a centuries-old tradition that doctors do not criticize each other openly. When this code of conduct was included in the Hippocratic Oath in the fifth century BC, doctors were required and expected to abide by strict standards of behavior. Originally, the rationale for this tradition was to ensure the public's confidence in doctors, a vital element in the process of healing and well-being, and to protect doctors from the many competing charlatans of that time. While today's doctors have ignored and rejected many traditions and expectations, one of the only traditions they have stuck to is that of protecting colleagues; there is a climate of "see no evil." This tradition has actually evolved into a code of silence, which has protected judgment errors, substandard care, and malpractice. The codes of medical ethics, both written and unwritten, neither imply nor require that one doctor covers for the mistakes of another; indeed, responsible behavior dictates the exact opposite. A new culture of carelessness and indifference to what is happening will continue to grow and develop, unless we do something to stop it. The excuses publically enumerated to justify this indifference are simply not good enough. However, while it is uncommon for doctors to overtly criticize one another, it is not unusual for them to give different advice to patients—in essence, disagreeing with colleagues. The multiple treatment options currently available are used to justify significant disagreements, which can sometimes confuse patients.

Changing Priorities

Over the last several decades, a significant shift in health care priorities has taken place. It is difficult not to notice the priority given to the convenience of doctors and hospitals over patients' well-being and welfare. Quality has been sacrificed for quantity. Long waits in doctors' offices, busy phone lines, and unavailable operating rooms (ORs), particularly for urgent cases, are proof of this dramatic shift away from prioritizing patients' health and well-being. Post-op patients are seen only when there is an opening in their surgeons' schedules, not necessarily when the patient requests to be seen. Doctors' secretaries have the last word on the date of a follow-up visit, irrespective of the patient's needs or the risks involved in delaying an exam or procedure. To protect themselves and their doctors, secretaries offer generic recommendations to patients who request to be seen for questions or complaints after surgery, or tell them to go to the emergency room (ER) if necessary. The long hours of waiting and the substandard care ERs tend to offer for non-life-threatening conditions is no secret.

As a doctor and a patient, I found that administrators' priorities are focused on "selling" services—often unnecessary hospital amenities that don't really improve care, such as window and room furnishings. Like most of my colleagues and patients, I prefer that other issues, more directly related to quality of care, be considered first. For example, long waits in doctors' offices and emergency rooms are inconvenient to patients, and doctors do not spend enough time with patients (often as little as five to ten minutes). Long hours of waiting in doctors' offices are not uncommon, and patients are usually not given any explanation or apology for delays.

For example, I was once waiting in my urologist's office along with three other patients. After an hour, the doctor appeared, walked through the waiting room, and left the office without acknowledging any of us. When I asked the secretary why the doctor had left, she told me it was because of "an emergency surgery." The emergency nature of the surgery may or may not have been true, but surgeries are more lucrative than routine visits, and as such, often take priority. Neither the doctor nor his secretary felt the obligation to explain to any of us what was happening or to apologize. This may not happen frequently, but there is no doubt that often, especially in clinics, patients do not always get the attention they deserve.

Other issues, such as understaffing of nurses and even telephone operators, are also pressing and have not been addressed with sincerity. For example, a new technology used in one Boston hospital automatically transfers patients' calls that are not answered in a timely manner from the nursing station to the cell phone of the on-duty head nurse. This supposed "improvement" ignores the fact that nurses and aides are often in the midst of helping other patients when calls come in, and that the head nurse is usually the busiest, particularly on our often-understaffed hospital floors.

Again, I can give personal examples of experiencing nursing understaffing as a patient as well as doctor. I was once an inpatient at MGH after a complicated orthopedics procedure. I rang the nurse for a sleeping pill at 11:00 p.m. No response, so I rang again at midnight. When I got no response by 1:00 a.m., I raised my voice. The nurse ran to my room apologizing. She explained that she was the only nurse on the floor and was busy with a patient who had had a cardiac arrest, hence her late arrival. I did not question her, but expressed my surprise that she could not get the extra help she needed, and that such a prestigious hospital allows such a critical understaffing. Addressing the understaffing issue would be a better preventive way to solve this problem. However, the complaints from both doctors and patients go ignored, because administrators "know best."

Medical Errors

Medical errors—causing death, disease, and suffering—are a serious national problem. The term "medical errors" encompasses a large variety of undesirable occurrences during the delivery of health care, and vary from harmless to fatal in their ultimate results. They include, among others, judgment and medication errors, unrecognized significant symptoms or signs, equipment malfunctions, and hospital-acquired infections and complications. Errors point to failures of the system and of the personnel involved.

Hospitals that cut corners in an effort to reduce costs unavoidably decrease the quality of care (although they claim otherwise), which leads to an increased risk of errors. Leadership in the medical profession is guilty of not striving to correct observed medical misbehaviors and recognizing the seriousness of new trends in the current practice of medicine. Currently, the main focus in medicine is on the bottom line and on patient volume; other noble aims of the profession, including quality and cost, are being sidelined. Doctors who may not have all the time needed for their patients have accepted this situation as an unavoidable reality. In such a setting, mistakes should not be considered unexpected surprises. Too much work and stress on quantity rather than quality are conducive to problems and errors. Patients tend to turn the other cheek when they witness or experience poor care, in order to avoid hassles. It is no surprise, therefore, that medical errors continue to occur by the thousands, and that problems of health care remain unsolved and even worsen.

According to a 1999 report from the Institute of Medicine, medical errors in the United States are blamed for up to ninety-eight thousand deaths and over a million patient injuries every year. In 2001, the University of Michigan found that only a tiny percentage of the deaths attributed to medical errors in the report could be attributed directly to mistakes.[8] Another study in 2004 suggested that the number of hospital patients who died from preventable errors may be twice as high as previously estimated, and found no evidence that patients' safety had improved over the last five years[9], since the infamous report of the Institute of Medicine. If proven true, these findings would make medical mistakes the third leading cause of death in the United States, behind heart disease and cancer, but ahead of car accidents and AIDS.

What is shocking is that the 1999 error figures elicited almost no response from the leadership in the medical profession, and no serious reforms were initiated after its release. It is a fact of life that recurring events that affect large groups of people get more attention than minor and isolated ones. One casualty in a car accident does not get the attention that two hundred casualties in a plane crash get. But no significant reactions followed the estimated possible ninety-eight thousand deaths in the United States from medical errors each year; alarms needed to be sounded, but they weren't. Business continued as usual, as if quality health care was no longer the responsibility of the health care industry. Medical doctors continued their routine practice unaffected. Legislators did not react with the intensity one would have expected. Medical administrators and bureaucrats reacted, but came up with solutions that did not reflect the importance or gravity of the situation, and that have had no significant effect to date. (The modest attempts at reform by administrators and insurance companies will be discussed in chapter 2.)

There is no evidence thus far that the number of errors has decreased significantly since the release of the report in 1999. Major causes of errors, like the shortage of nurses, assembly-line clinics, inadequate student teaching, and unsupervised residents remain unaddressed. Unless these are addressed, errors are likely to continue to occur.

Debates about the exact number of deaths due to errors are not really that important and need not consume a lot of energy and funds. What is important is that deaths and injuries do occur in exceedingly high numbers because of avoidable mistakes, and that the preventive and corrective measures adopted so far have not had a noticeable effect. This is a very serious issue, and efforts must first be directed toward reducing

---

8   Kimberly Atkins, "Study Revisits Medical Error Deaths," *Boston Globe*, July 25, 2001.

9   Scott Allen, "Higher Toll Cited from Hospital Errors," *Boston Globe*, July 27, 2004.

errors. Subsequently, systems should be devised to monitor progress and ensure that improvement follows. The individuals involved should not be exonerated on the assumption that errors are always system failures (see chapter 9 for more on this theme).

The Quality of Health Care in America Committee of the Institute of Medicine formulated an ambitious and comprehensive ten-year strategy aimed at avoiding medical errors. The plan, published in the 2001 book *Crossing the Quality Chasm: A New Health System for the 21st Century*, includes the creation of a national center for patient safety, a mandatory reporting system, and an increased Federal Drug Administration (FDA) and hospital involvement in preventing medication errors. It also stresses the necessity of performance standards focused more on patient safety and suggests that professional societies play a much more active role in improving patient care. Very few of these recommendations have been adopted to date, and little improvement has been documented so far.

To the best of my knowledge, the only significant progress achieved since the publication of the plan involves the reduction of hospital medication errors, including such categories as wrong patient, wrong drug, wrong dose, and wrong time. An automated medication monitoring system has already been credited for a significant decrease in serious medication errors. Pharmacists and nurses must be credited for their efforts and the results they have already achieved. Unfortunately, no significant progress on other fronts has been made so far.

The recommendations of the Institute of Medicine are certainly comprehensive and ambitious. They look most impressive on paper, but unfortunately they may not be particularly practical or even accomplishable. They rely too heavily on correcting systems and creating new ones—which boils down to unnecessary additional layers of bureaucracy, with all that this implies. The report does not appear to put enough stress on the role of individuals, on the role of teaching and supervising students and trainees, and on the role of continuing medical education. Additionally, for even the most egregious errors, the only punishment proposed or implied in the report is financial.

As I will advocate in chapter 9, avoidable and repetitive mistakes of medical practitioners deserve to be exposed and punished as an additional step in preventing medical errors. Avoidable medical errors can occur at any stage of patient management, and the people who commit errors should be held accountable. It is neither the health care system nor the hospital that are responsible when a doctor makes a mistake. What preventive measures could administrators mandate to prevent spine surgeons from operating on the wrong disk or the wrong vertebra? Ultimately, this is a responsibility nobody can assume except the surgeon. If the surgeons stopped over-scheduling cases because of either pressure or greed, they would have the time to be more careful and make fewer mistakes. Some surgeons feel that they are protected by the reputation and fame of the large teaching hospitals and famous medical schools that employ them; otherwise, they wouldn't allow themselves to be so lax.

Doctors at fault should be publicly sanctioned or disciplined and required to pay out of pocket for their negligence. I do not see the wisdom of having the insurance companies assume all the cost of errors and their consequences. The out-of-pocket costs would motivate doctors to be more careful.

The unwritten policy of cover-ups and the tradition of secrecy among health care providers are often tolerated, even expected, and may be discreetly encouraged by administrators and lawyers to avoid the possibility of bad publicity and risky lawsuits. This attitude is no secret among doctors and other health care providers, but is rarely admitted and discussed openly.

Performing surgical procedures outside of one's area of training and expertise is yet another reason errors occur, a fact that is well known but seems to be tolerated. For example, the ear, nose, and throat (ENT) surgeons who adopted in the late '80s the popular endoscopic sinus surgery techniques for the surgical treatment of chronic sinus disorders, without adequate training, were responsible for a number of serious results, including blindness and death (see chapter 8). Primary care doctors who are not specifically trained in reading EKGs or evaluating eardrums simply should not attempt to do either. Allergists who are not trained in intranasal examination should not treat nasal polyps without appropriate consultations. Inadequate supervision of trainees is common; interns and residents are often put to work to generate business for the hospital. Reliance on paramedical personnel is also increasing, as a way to free up the more expensive time of doctors so they can generate more income.

The Institute for Healthcare Improvement has close to four thousand hospitals nationwide enlisted to protect patients from medical errors. Yet, when known causes of errors are not addressed, how much success can be hoped for? Most of the errors I have witnessed occurred when doctors saw more patients than is optimal, surgeons performed operations they had not been trained to do, and residents went unsupervised in emergency rooms.

I see no evidence that these issues have been comprehensively addressed yet in the campaign to reduce errors.

My observations throughout this book are not unique to my own working environment. They are widespread across the nation. All of the colleagues I consulted with while preparing this book shared similar or worse experiences. The fact that these issues occur in prestigious hospitals, like the one I worked in, and leading universities, like the one where I taught, points to a major failure of leadership in these institutions. In order for things to change, we need to reestablish a responsible code of conduct for doctors and their leaders so that they may step up and qualify to take responsibility for a new, universal health care plan. A serious, comprehensive reform is imperative at many levels and in many fields of health care.

Chapter Two
Health Care Reform

Millions of Americans have no health insurance, tens of thousands of deaths occur from medical errors each year, and health care costs continue to escalate at an alarming rate. While none of these issues have gone unnoticed, none of them have been perceived as important enough to be seriously addressed and solved. Needed reform is slow to come to the U.S. health and insurance industries. Of the reforms adopted by the U.S. government thus far, most have only served as Band-Aids: they have failed to improve or slow the worsening health landscape (as the statistics clearly show); they have done little to curb medical errors; and they have failed to put patients' well-being before that of insurance companies, pharmaceutical companies, and hospitals. Rather than being proactive, Congress reacts to issues that garner national attention. Past reforms have been selected and prioritized by insurance companies, hospitals, and regulators, mainly to serve their own agendas. For the most part, the medical profession has been remarkably absent from the reform movement. Some of the costly reforms currently in place make sense, but have yet to prove their value—and many may turn out to be completely ineffective. Unfortunately, reforms are often pitched as advancing the national economy (for example, investments in costly technological advances), rather than carried out as sincere efforts to fix health care delivery. In other words, too often the focus is on the byproducts of reform, rather than its true aims.

History of Health Care Reform in the United States

For more than half a century, the U.S. government has tried unsuccessfully to become directly involved with health care reform. The first serious attempt was in 1945, when President Truman wanted to pass a compulsory universal health insurance law, but he failed. Powerful corporations, including the American Medical Association (AMA), campaigned against him, because they feared the law would socialize medicine. Indeed, to this day socialization continues to be perceived as un-American. The AMA claimed in its campaigns against Truman's proposals that it was attempting to preserve patients' and doctors' freedom to choose one another, but in reality, it focused mainly on doctors' interests.

President Nixon in 1974, President Carter in 1979, and President Clinton in 1995 each put forth proposals to broaden health insurance coverage and make it universal. Each of their proposed plans would have mandated employers to provide health insurance to their employees—on the company's own dime. All the proposals brought to the table by these presidents were killed by businesses.

Despite Medicare's reputation as one of the better-managed health insurance providers in the United States, it is far from perfect. It certainly has not contributed to the creation of a pleasant and efficient medical practice atmosphere. Its rules are complicated and keep changing, as we shall see later in the book. Medicare has no effective system to monitor compliance; as a result, a report by the inspector general at the department of Health and Human Services found an error rate of almost 29 percent in a sample of claims paid in 2006 under Medicare's multibillion-dollar durable medical equipment program (which provides equipment like wheelchairs).[10] Of the estimated $400 billion budgeted for Medicare in 2008, $70 billion may disappear due to fraud and mismanagement.[11]

The medical profession's passivity has given government bureaucrats and hospital administrators the exclusive responsibility to apply, interpret, monitor, and adjust to Medicare's continuously changing regulations. Hospital administrators are good at finding ways to go around regulations and cover up their tracks when they do not respect them; they strictly respect the counsel of their lawyers to ensure they stay within the law and avoid lawsuits.

Universal, government-run health care remains a casualty of political realities. Market forces are hard to oppose in our capitalist, free-market system; corporations are immune to changes that do not favor them, and

10 Christopher Lee, "Report Faults Medicare Audits," *Washington Post*, August 26, 2008.

11 Lyric Wallwork Winik and Stephen Dignan, "Intelligence Report," *Parade*, April 20, 2008.

"rationing" care is un-American. Raising taxes—one way of financing universal health care—is unpopular, especially during election campaigns.

Given these obstacles, there are currently two prevailing ideas in health care reform discussions. The first is to create systems that improve care and aim at preventing errors—but that do not address the individuals who commit the errors. This emphasis is due in part to the Institute of Medicine's notorious reports on medical errors. The second prevailing idea is that we need to be able to measure a problem before we can fix it; therefore, "measuring" health care results is a requirement for reform. I think these ideas need to be debated further and tested, before we base our reforms around them. I disagree with these ideas as cornerstones of reform, which I believe needs to be multifaceted and presented as a package deal. Reform cannot be effective if it is introduced piecemeal. In the following sections, I'll examine some of the major reform trends, organizations, and laws.

Organizations and Professional Associations

There are a variety of government organizations and professional associations that have at least attempted reform. I'll detail both nationwide initiatives, including those by quality improvement organizations, and the Accreditation Council for Graduate Medical Education, and the Institute for Healthcare Improvement, and those by Massachusetts-based organizations, such as the Massachusetts Hospital Association (MHA).

Quality improvement organizations are a little-known network of private contractors. There is one organization in every state, plus Puerto Rico and the U.S. Virgin Islands. Medicare contracts their services to measure and improve hospital care and to investigate patients' complaints. It is unfortunate that the law allows them to operate in secrecy, so plaintiffs have no access to their deliberations and conclusions. Their findings and recommendations are not available to the complainers and to the public. The majority of their board members are medical doctors, and their executives are very well paid, receiving $200,000 to $300,000 per year.

Over the years, their mission has shifted from inspection and regulation to collaborating with hospitals and doctors to improve care, two not-very-compatible aims. They operate under the debatable premise that problems are better addressed by cooperation, rather than discipline, and that problems are caused by systems, not doctors or hospitals.[12]

---

12 Gilbert M. Gaul, "Chronic Condition: Medicare's Oversight Gaps," *Washington Post*, July 26, 2005.

The astronomically high number of deaths per year from medical errors reported by the Institute of Medicine testifies to these and other similar regulatory organizations' failures to perform their tasks effectively. The $300 million that Medicare pays for quality improvement organizations' services has not proved to be a justified or worthwhile investment.

Other organizations' efforts to improve health care have been similarly undermined by the emphasis on "cooperation" and "systemic flaws." For example, campaigns by the Institute for Healthcare Improvement have failed to attain their goals. The Institute for Healthcare Improvement is an independent, not-for-profit organization that aims to lead health care improvement throughout the world. It was founded in 1991 in Cambridge, Massachusetts. In 2004, it launched the 100,000 Lives Campaign in the U.S. The campaign gave itself eighteen months to achieve its goal of improving patient safety and saving lives. All U.S. hospitals were invited to join in implementing the campaign and documenting interventions, but less than half of all U.S. hospitals joined in the initial stages. This campaign represents an important effort by an independent organization to improve the quality and the safety of health care, but it is worth noting that this and similar projects assume that the quality and safety of health care are mainly a hospital's responsibility, and not a doctor's. Since it is primarily doctors who are responsible for the well-being of their patients, the final results of such campaigns will likely be discouraging and their expenses unjustifiable, unless doctors become actively involved.

The Alternative Quality Contract (AQC) is a Blue Cross Blue Shield of Massachusetts initiative introduced in 2007. In this contract, payments are to be based on quality, outcome, and efficiency rather than on patient volume and the complexity of the services provided. Doctors' and hospitals' payments are to be based on quality and outcome versus quantity of care. AQC includes two forms of payments, one fixed per patient, and one with a substantial performance incentive tied to quality, effectiveness, and patient satisfaction. It is assumed that over time, this contract will help improve health care quality dramatically and reduce medical costs, but there is no proof so far that it can achieve either claim.

The idea of rewarding doctors for their success in treating patients is certainly a good one, but to measure success and assess quality of care simply by reviewing records to make sure all the tests judged necessary by insurers and bureaucrats were ordered on time and the appropriate protocols were strictly followed is a wrong and unfair oversimplification of a much more complex issue. It is well known that appropriate care may be different for different patients suffering from similar conditions. A patient's race, age, cultural background, outlook on life, lifestyle, and health status all play a role in decision making and management planning. Additionally, a patient may not always follow a doctor's advice. In this case, doctors should not be penalized for the delinquency of their patients.

I doubt that success and quality of care can ever be measured fairly by reviewing medical records. Insurance companies, regulatory agencies, and businesses insist on data measurement, but actual outcomes are not always measurable. For example, hypertension and diabetes—often used to explain and illustrate the greatness of this system—are amenable to outcome studies (the aim is a measurable, normal blood pressure and a measurable, normal sugar level in the blood). But other diagnoses, like headache, dizziness, back and abdominal pains, and psychiatric disorders are not that easily amenable and measurable, if at all.

AQC is, in fact, masterminded by insurance companies and supported by hospital corporations. It serves their purposes first and foremost. It allows them to stay in control and to adjust payments to fit their budgets and fiscal aims. The use of this and similar outcome studies can only result in increasing the grip of insurance companies and hospitals on health care. The studies justify the use of all or some of the collected data to dictate reimbursement levels. They also give large hospitals an advantage over smaller hospitals and private practices that cannot afford all of the costly resources needed to implement and monitor outcome studies in order to prove compliance to regulators. We have already seen small practices and small hospitals disappear from the health care scene, because they cannot afford the resources needed to comply and compete.

The Accreditation Council for Graduate Medical Education (ACGME) is another organization that attempts to correct the high prevalence of medical errors. In 2003, ACGME imposed guidelines for residents' working hours. Currently, residents work a maximum of eighty hours per week, take one full day off per week, and have at least ten hours off between shifts. They cannot work more than a thirty-hour shift, and if they do work one, the last six hours of the shift may not be devoted to any clinical care. ACGME's idea is to give residents a better quality of life, reduce the incidence of medical errors, and hopefully create better doctors.

This policy constitutes a major change to an old tradition. During my days of residency at the American University of Beirut, we were on duty at the hospital every other night and weekend. Working thirty-six continuous hours was not unheard of. In the Halsted surgical training program at the

Johns Hopkins Hospital, which I joined in 1965, interns and residents were on call twenty-four hours a day, seven days a week, eleven months a year. The twelfth month was a vacation. The idea behind the strictness of the program was to help make good doctors with strong characters, able to work long hours even under adverse conditions. Did we commit mistakes because of these requirements? Probably, but an adequate supervision system and the availability of seniors for consultations made the risk low. More errors naturally occur when young trainees are left to work alone and expected to do more work than optimal—and that danger is present even in the current thirty-hour shifts. In spite of this new policy, the risk of errors is greater because so many training programs are understaffed and because more stress is put on productivity, rather than on education and proper supervision. In sum, these measures are a step in the right direction, but they don't address the much more serious problems of the lessening commitment to medical teaching.

In January 2005, Patients First, a voluntary program designed to improve patient safety in 105 Massachusetts hospitals, was started. The program is sponsored by the Massachusetts Hospital Association (MHA) and the Massachusetts Organization of Nurse Executives (MONE). (Note the absence of medical doctors from the program's sponsors.) Its five aims are as follows:

1. Inform patients, their families, and the public about safe staffing.
2. Promote a supportive work environment in which safety is a top priority.
3. Require hospitals to report their own performances on a series of nationally recognized safety and quality measurements.
4. Offer nurses in-house education, such as mentoring opportunities and scholarship programs.
5. Educate the public about how quality and safety can be improved.[13]

The program's aims are noble, but in practice, it generates more rules, data, reports, costs, and bureaucracy. Will it improve standards of care? Will it improve patients' safety? Will it help solve the nurse shortage problem? These are relevant questions that will probably remain unanswered. Hospital administrators are good at generating and launching costly, impractical programs that look good on paper and work well in

13 Massachusetts Patients First Program, "Patient Care Link," accessed October 11, 2010, http://www.patientcarelink.org/about-patientcarelink/our-mission.aspx.

PR campaigns, but the wisdom and effectiveness of such programs are doubtful.

Most glaringly, the program ignores the heavy workload of nurses—an issue that urgently needs to be addressed. The current nursing shortage could best be eased with a pay increase. By diverting some of the money available in the system that currently goes to insurance companies, pharmaceutical companies, health care administrators, and overpaid executives, there would be enough money to cover this necessary expense. This is just one example of how ivory tower administrators try to improve a system without consulting the men and women on the front line, namely the practicing doctors and nurses.

Reform Trends

Reforms in the recent past have focused on "measuring medicine" (as in evidence-based medicine), "improving the system" (as in technological reforms), and "consolidation" (as in the idea of salaried doctors and hospital conglomerates).

Technology can play an important part in reforms. Ambitious, "futuristic" technological ideas and projects to improve health care include the following: putting all the medications a patient needs into one pill; implanting computers into a patient that can be programmed from a distance to change doses and record vital signs; and performing increasingly complex invasive procedures and surgeries using robots. Technological ideas that are already being tested or implemented include electronic records, bar codes to reduce the risk of medication errors, patient ID wristbands for cross-checking medications orders, and handheld scanners that ensure at the end of an operation that all sponges are accounted for and none forgotten in a body cavity. Though technology has already been introduced in many health care reform efforts, the results and benefits have been unclear—while the costs have been astronomical. Some of the above ideas are futuristic and exciting, but whether they can improve care while keeping it affordable remains to be seen. For example, the jury is still out about the worth of robotic prostate surgery. The major technological and medical advances that we have witnessed over the last few decades have benefited many, but have also raised costs, leaving more people unable to afford health insurance.

The first problem with many of these technological solutions is that they aim to address medical errors when far cheaper solutions would be more effective. For example, the idea of using handheld scanners to scan for sponges is meant to prevent the serious current problem of instruments and supplies being inadvertently left in operative sites. In Florida (where medical error reporting is required by law) in 2001, 122 surgical procedures were performed to remove foreign bodies left in patients after surgery, along with fifty-four wrong site procedures, sixteen wrong procedures, and nine procedures on wrong patients.[14] It is not only "idiots" who commit mistakes, but even smart surgeons. When surgeons are finishing an operation, nurses may be answering phones while doing sponge counts, and everybody is in a hurry; mistakes do happen.

However, the whole problem of medical errors would be better handled from another angle—that of preventing their causes, such as operating room understaffing and surgeons' work overloads. These are not impossible problems to solve, but unfortunately, they have not been given priority. It is simpler for administrators and regulators to go around them and create more rules and use technology—technology that is often sold to them by aggressive marketers. On that subject, it's worth noting that it is neither safe nor wise to allow costly, innovative medical research to remain under the control of entrepreneurs and for-profit industries. Aggressive salesmanship usually succeeds in selling anything new, under the popular assumption that it is superior to what is already available—an assumption that is not always correct, and that will be explored in greater depth in chapter 7.

As another example, computer systems have been introduced to help solve the serious chronic problem of hospital medication errors, of which there were an estimated 430,000 in 1992, and 17,000 of which affected patient care outcome.[15] Hospitals are being pressured to replace handwritten ordering systems with electronic ones. These systems seem very promising, but even their proponents admit a lot of work still needs to be done to make them function well; proof is still lacking that the new systems save lives and reduce costs. Moreover, while this system may help reduce the number of medication errors, it does not prevent nor address doctors' errors in ordering and prescribing medications.

Above all, the hefty price tag for computerized medication systems is

---

14   Samuel C. Seiden and Paul Barach, "Wrong-Side/Wrong-Site, Wrong-Procedure, and Wrong-Patient Adverse Events: Are They Preventable?" *JAMA* 141 (September 2006), http://archsurg.ama-assn.org /cgi/ reprint/141/9/931.pdf.

15   C.A. Bond, C.L. Raehl, and T. Franke, "Medication Errors in United States Hospitals," *Pharmacotherapy: The Journal of Human Pharmacology and Drug Therapy* 21, no. 9 (2001): 1023-1036.

a cause for concern. The systems include expensive hardware that must be purchased up front and recurring, monthly equipment upkeep charges. Additionally, software for the databases needs to be purchased from other vendors, who update the systems monthly as new drugs are added. Similar systems have also proven costly. For example, in 2006, Brigham and Women's Hospital in Boston acquired a barcode system for medications, paying ten million dollars for equipment and training. Additional yearly maintenance fees will have to be paid.

A third problem is that Congress has yet to regulate this industry. Vendors have standard contracts, which relieve them of all liabilities in case something goes wrong. The dangers of such lack of regulation have been illustrated to me by personal experience; I know of a fatality that occurred because the nurse on duty one night was not aware that the code needed to access the medications cart had been changed. She was unable to obtain the emergency medication in time.

I don't mean to imply, however, than technological change is without value. To be fair, electronic health records (EHRs) represent an excellent addition to health care; they contribute to improving both its quality and efficiency. The advantages of EHRs are numerous: there is no need to repeatedly reenter patient information like demographics, allergies, or medications; doctors have fast and easy access to all patient information previously entered; no physical storage space is needed for files; the chronic, frustrating, and time-consuming problem of interpreting illegible doctor handwriting and waiting for the records from the records room are resolved; important information, like serious allergies, bleeding disorders, adverse drug interactions, or a family history of malignant hyperthermia following general anesthesia, can be flagged to attract fast attention; and there's no more need for medical records departments to deliver records to clinics, emergency rooms, and hospitals under time constraints. They also facilitate our complicated reimbursement process. The availability of voice recording technologies has facilitated the process of doctors entering information into EHRs without the need to learn typing skills, and has saved on the expenses needed for transcriptionists.

EHRs are so far still an institutional endeavor and not a national requirement. For example, health care providers in every Partners HealthCare facility in Massachusetts have access to all information on patients who present for medical attention in any of Partners' facilities. Hopefully the system will reach its maximum potential when all medical records are integrated into one national program. It remains to be seen, however, whether or not this system will also contribute to controlling costs. I personally doubt it, because of the business nature of the current health care delivery.

Those who champion the importance and value of EHR systems, however, assume that doctors always read available records. But from personal experience, I know that many do not, especially when they are overbooked, delayed in their clinics, or have already decided that the recorded information is not relevant to the patient's presenting complaints. For example, I once went to see an orthopedist for tennis elbow. He focused on my elbow, and never looked at the computer monitor. I was in and out in five minutes. I considered that experience a poor practice, which no technological advances can possibly help.

While EHR has yet to become broadly-based, other reform trends are focusing on consolidation, as in not-for-profit hospital conglomerates. These entities are relative newcomers in the health care field. They are becoming powerful entities that are concerned with their own interests and protection. They significantly marginalize medical doctors by making medical decisions (as will be outlined in chapter 5).

For example, Partners HealthCare of Massachusetts is one of these conglomerates. It was founded in secrecy in 1993 by Massachusetts General and Brigham and Women's hospitals, two major flagships of Harvard Medical School.[16] Partners' mission is to achieve "an integrated health care system that offers patients a continuum of coordinated high quality care."[17] When it was conceived, it was supposed to save hundreds of millions of dollars by consolidating two famous Boston hospitals. This aim was never achieved, and Partners eventually became a driving force behind the high cost of medicine in Massachusetts.[18]

Partners quickly grew to become the second-largest employer in Massachusetts, after the state itself. Its offices are in one of the most expensive buildings in downtown Boston, and it is run like a corporation,

---

16 It was reported that the medical dean of the Ivy League of the school with which these two hospitals are affiliated learned of the conglomerate's foundation while reading the newspaper one morning. The dean had been considering ways to bring together all of the hospitals affiliated with Harvard under the umbrella of Harvard Medical School, but was trumped by Partners.

17 "Our Partners & Collaborators," Massachusetts Coalition of School-Based Health Centers, http://www .mcsbhc.org/partners.php.

18 Scott Allen and others, "A Handshake That Made Healthcare History," *Boston Globe*, December 28, 2008.

with highly paid executives and an ambition for growth. Through unfair competition, Partners has acquired smaller Massachusetts health enterprises struggling to survive. For example, in 2000, it discreetly struck a deal with Blue Cross Blue Shield of Massachusetts to receive $193 million over three years as a compensation for its previous low rates. This deal was never put on paper, since it represented possible violations of antitrust laws and use of market power to fix or increase prices and exercise unfair competition. The dominant headline of the *Boston Globe* of December 28, 2008, read appropriately, "A Handshake That Made Healthcare History." The report stated that Partners had become "big enough to overwhelm competitors and intimidate insurers."[19] Indeed, Partners currently is a giant; as such, it dictates its own terms. For example, in 2000, it received from Blue Cross Blue Shield a 75 percent increase in its reimbursements. The insurer prospered too, gaining more members and watching profits soar from $82.7 million in 2002, to more than $200 million a year in each of the next five years.[20] Whether health care conglomerates are a sad or a happy development for health care remains to be seen, but I suspect they will prove to be a sad development. The power insurance companies managed to acquire in health care has not had a positive influence. For that reason, I'm concerned about another dominating giant, run like a corporation, developing in health care.

Another risky reform move has been the rise in the number of salaried doctors. Salaried positions are a double-edged sword. Hospitals offer salaries compatible with national averages, which helps reduce the large difference in income for different specialties, and is likely to encourage more doctors to become primary care physicians (PCPs), a position currently understaffed nationwide. Also, salaried doctors don't have to worry about the administrative headaches of running their own practices.

That said, the increasing trend of salaried doctors has had negative consequences on several fronts. First, salaries for doctors make the practice of fee splitting by hospital administrators easier—at doctors' expense. This fee splitting is, of course, discreet and not named as such. The 2000 edition of the *American Heritage Medical Dictionary* defines fee splitting as "the practice of sharing fees with professional colleagues, such as physicians, for patient or client referrals." In essence, what occurs is that hospitals that employ full-time doctors tax the extra income doctors generate over

19   Ibid.

20   Ibid.

their cost centers. The justification offered is that the patients a doctor sees in his hospital clinic are the hospital's patients, not the doctor's. This assumption is not always correct, because many doctors acquire independent reputations and attract patients regardless of the hospital at which they work.

In addition to fee splitting, salaried doctors are more vulnerable to losing some of their identity and independence, elements traditionally considered vital in the practice of medicine. As a result, administrators then play a bigger decision-making role in health care. For example, they can require doctors to see more patients, and they can take away administrative control by dictating that medical secretaries will be employed by hospitals rather than the doctors themselves. Such decision-making power is risky, as will be outlined in chapter 5. Also, if doctors know that they will be paid the same, no matter how well they perform their jobs, some of them may not have enough motivation to do their best, unless an incentive plan is built in. Finally, while doctors' incomes will drop on average, there is little proof that overall health care costs will decrease as a result. It is more likely that hospitals will pocket the saved money.

Another risky trend in health care reform is so-called evidence-based medicine (EBM), which is the use of current, best scientific evidence to make decisions about the care of individual patients. EBM integrates doctors' clinical experience and expertise with the available external clinical evidence from systematic research. Ideally, in EBM, doctors and patients pick an option which is most appropriate for the specific case by making use of statistics and probabilities. For example, evidence-based guidelines state that spine surgery for chronic lower back pain has a 60 percent chance of success, as does physical therapy, while acupuncture allows a 40 percent chance for improvement. EBM suggests that patients and doctors choose an option with these numbers in mind.

EBM is a movement that grew to help doctors make rational management decisions, and to guide third-party payers in decisions about which treatments are coverable by insurance and which ones are not. EBM seems to be a good idea at first glance, but it can be dangerous over time. For example, in the current practice of medicine, there are many treatment options available for many diseases, each with proponents and adversaries. This fact can be confusing to patients and medical students. Nor are optimal double-blind, placebo-controlled studies to evaluate these options always feasible, ethical, or practical.

Moreover, EBM may encourage abuses by doctors who believe that the practice of medicine is solely a business for profit. Conflicts of interest in the scientific process are inevitable, given the aggressive marketing of the pharmaceutical industry and the large number of doctors on pharmaceutical payrolls as consultants. Indeed, opponents of EBM are concerned that it may eventually encourage empirical quackery in medical practice. Evidence-based individual decisions (EBIDs) rely on the experience and expertise of one doctor, and on the level of trust he or she inspires in patients.

Above all, the problem with EBM is that it ignores the fact that many aspects of medical care are influenced by individual factors and values that vary and are not measurable by scientific methods. Such factors include the patient's age, general health, lifestyle, values, and outlook on life values, which all play important roles in decision making.

Patient Safety

In 1999, the Institute of Medicine issued a landmark study on the prevalence of medical errors. Since then, a new focus has been on creating an institutional culture for quality and safety for patients and employees. Unfortunately, the result has often been only pro forma reforms. Many of these reforms rest on the assumption, like evidence-based medicine, that you cannot change what you cannot measure. This assumption does not always apply. Measurements of health care outcomes may not prove to be always possible or fair in the long run.

One of the major reform efforts in the early 2000s has been initiated by the same Institute of Medicine committee that issued the 1999 landmark report on medical errors. In its report of 2001, this committee advocated a totally new system for health care.[21] It recommended a sweeping redesign of the American health care system and provided overarching principles for specific direction for policy makers and others involved in health care. This redesign fell under the following four headings:

1. Performance expectations for the twenty-first century.
2. Rules to guide patient-clinician relationships.
3. Frameworks to better align the incentives inherent in payments with improvements in quality.

---

21 Institute of Medicine, *Crossing the Quality Chasm: A New Health System for the Twenty-first Century* (Washington DC: National Academy Press, 2001).

4. Promotion of evidence-based medicine and strengthening of clinical information systems.

The report called on Congress to appropriate one billion dollars to support projects aimed at making health care safer, more scientifically based, more equitable, and more efficient. To the best of my knowledge, this report is not currently on the discussion tables. It probably continues to accumulate dust, along with previous reports and suggestions that had not pleased the powerful, capitalistic major health care players.

In July 2005, four years after the Institute of Health's proposed reforms were issued, Congress approved the Federal Patient Safety Quality Improvement Act, which seeks to create a national patient safety reporting system. Medical errors henceforth should be reported, and hospitals are required to study the reports and find solutions to help prevent them in the future. A federal network will be created to receive and analyze these reports and make sure that preventive measures are being adopted.

At first glance and on paper, this act seems appropriate, but closer examination reveals its weaknesses: the reporting is voluntary, and the information is protected and therefore cannot be used in litigations. It is no secret that doctors and hospitals prefer to cover their mistakes when they occur, if they can get away with it—which they often do. Experience has shown that public reporting in the media, for example, usually leads to more serious attention and corrective action, and less risk of cover-ups. This act provides an unjustified protection to individuals and institutions when they admit to committing a mistake, even if it has a criminal component.

Moreover, systems of reporting errors, whether required or voluntary, have not proven to be very effective. There are twenty-three states that already have laws regarding reporting medical errors. In Florida, where medical error reporting is required by law, a significant number of surgical errors still occurs.

These alarming figures prove the limited effectiveness of the present error-reporting laws, and provide further proof about the dismal failure of the medical profession in assuming its natural responsibilities in health care.

Experience has shown that any new system carries with it the risk of bringing in new and unexpected hazards and stresses. In the high-stress, fast-paced work environment of health care, the risk of errors will persist, perhaps to different degrees, no matter how much new technology is brought in. Why do we address only errors, the consequences of such a work environment, rather than the environment conducive to errors, which cry out for reform? We need to keep root causes in mind at all times when serious reform is on the table.

In contrast to the failure of external systems for reporting errors, mandated morbidity and mortality conferences in hospitals could be steps in the right direction, if properly conducted. I based this assertion on the belief that the only way to prevent errors is for the medical profession to assume the responsibility of seriously policing itself, rather than relying on external "policing."

However, the problem with morbidity and mortality conferences as they are presently formulated is that they fall short of full disclosure and accountability. Morbidity and mortality conferences are usually held monthly, and cover complications or deaths among patients who were admitted to the hospital or who underwent surgery. Thus, outpatients are not discussed. Those errors that do not result in complications are not reported, nor are they investigated. Additionally, time constraints do not allow the discussion of every reported complication; many complications remain covered up. Moreover, even errors that are discussed are usually not admitted and labeled as such, no matter how obvious they are, either in the discussions or in the confidential minutes. Though these conferences are a step in the right direction, the medical profession has yet to initiate an effective system of error reporting and prevention, nor does it seem to be braced to do so soon.

Obama's Reforms

I emphasize the problems on the ground with current trends and proposed health care reforms, because, when I watched the passionate debates on television about Obama's plan for health care reform, I was reminded just how out of touch and unaccountable our politicians in Washington are. In the fall of 2009, for example, I remember that a member of Congress suggested that the first step in reform should be to find out whether or not we can afford it. He was advocating fixing the current system, rather than changing it.

But the basic issue on the table is not whether industries will benefit or suffer from reform, whether we can afford reform or not, or whether socialism is a bad word or not. The issue is that 15 percent of our population is uninsured, and the number is growing. This should not be acceptable in the United States. Capitalism has failed health care for decades—and continues to do so. Why do we continue to abide by capitalist health care with so much passion and force? In the country with the biggest economy in the world, questions about whether we can "afford" universal health care should not have been brought up at all, especially given that less affluent, industrialized, capitalist countries have enjoyed universal health care for decades. We are witnessing an increased focus on funding sources and allocations, rather than on the ultimate aim of universal coverage—which is what matters in the end.

It is also unbelievable that congressmen generously supported by lobbies and oblivious to health care red flags are tolerated and reelected by their constituents, while they try to maintain the status quo in a failing system, whose only beneficiaries are special interests. They continue to assume leadership responsibilities that they have proved to be unworthy of, and to block effective reform. Our democracy has failed health care. It is time we put national vanity aside and learn from other democracies that have long provided their citizens with universal health care.

Health care reform was not part of the mainstream political discussion until President Obama was elected. He should be credited for being persistent enough to bring it to center stage. Obama's ultimate noble and responsible aim is to have an affordable, equitable, and quality health care system for all Americans, including the forty-six million who currently cannot afford it.

Unfortunately, ideological arguments, party politics, and political polarization have blurred this ultimate aim. The conservative legislators who had successfully blocked universal health care on several occasions in the past have not been able to block it totally under Obama, because the majority of the American people want it. Indeed, the media has frequently reported that polls have revealed that 70 percent of the public and 65 percent of doctors favor a public option in the final health care reform bill. In a true democracy, these figures should be enough to pass Obama's bill. But the fight continues, indicating the power and influence of the companies that generously support lawmakers and finance powerful lobbyists. The virulence of the fight between liberals who want a public option and the conservatives who do not illustrates the severity of the dangerous polarization regarding health care currently taking place in the United States.

Paradoxically, in our democracy, it is not the majority that calls the shots in health care, but rather a powerful capitalist system. The fact that our system has failed in providing health care has not been given adequate attention and importance. A responsible capitalist system should not object to creating more competition among health insurance companies by offering a public option, and should force them to be accountable for their actions.

There have been no serious debates as of yet on the malpractice system, though they should be forthcoming. The fight for an effective malpractice reform to help control costs will probably be more difficult than the fight for universal health care, because the legal profession's interests will be diminished. But it is just as necessary and important.

Congress has acted courageously on more than one occasion in the past for the interests of the public—why not now? Not only did President Johnson succeeded in introducing Medicare and Medicaid in 1965, but Congress acted boldly by passing the Patriot Act after September 11, despite its unpopularity—and, arguably, its unconstitutionality. A universal health care plan is a must, and it is needed now. Hopefully it will happen under the Obama administration.

Chapter Three
Failing Leaders

Whether or not it is explicitly spelled out in their job descriptions, leaders in the medical field, as elsewhere, are expected to lead and hold themselves to high standards of conduct. Deans of medical schools, university department chairs, hospital CEOs and chiefs, and presidents of medical staffs are these leaders, as are medical society officers and the editors and editorial boards of medical journals. These are the medical leaders who impact the delivery of health care.

Unfortunately, these groups have failed to lead; instead, they follow trends, however unfavorable. I believe that leaders in the medical field carry a major responsibility for the failings of our profession and the subsequent health care crisis. They are missing in national debates on reform and major issues like abortion, stem cell research, gene therapy, and even medical education and training. They have allowed their priorities to be dictated by reimbursements and financial incentives, and have almost exclusively spent their time adjusting to the unfavorable changes imposed on medicine by outside forces, rather than preventing, resisting, or altering them.

Market forces have been allowed to play important and decisive roles in health care, with catastrophic results. Medical leaders have supported and even adopted business principles that were not designed for the practice of medicine or the management of suffering. The requirements of the body, the soul, and the psyche of a suffering human being cannot be adequately addressed by business principles. The trust, comfort, and support that a medical doctor provides a patient can be as important as the prescribed medications and the performed surgeries.

Leaders in the medical field have learned from administrators and others that the appearance of propriety is more important than propriety itself. The concept of right or wrong seems to no longer exist—almost any behavior to increase income and cut down expenses has become justifiable. For example, many leaders in the medical field choose the easy way of obtaining funding—accepting and encouraging donations from prosperous pharmaceutical companies—rather than working hard to secure the needed money from conflict-of-interest-free sources.

Medical school deans, department chairs, and hospital chiefs possess and exercise tremendous power. They successfully hide, when they want to and when it is convenient, behind the committees, rules, and regulations that they have accepted or initiated. They are accountable on paper, but that accountability is only pro forma. They are not sufficiently regulated; their performances are neither regularly monitored nor seriously evaluated. These leaders do not encourage criticism from within, and unfortunately are not the potential source of change and improvement in the medical profession that they are supposed to be.

It is true that today's medicine is too complex to allow medical leaders alone to continue to call most of the shots in health care. Financial, ethical, legal, and moral issues have become important and require the advice of experts—but not necessarily their rulings. However, leaders have significantly turned their backs on the traditions that have earned medical doctors the respected and privileged positions they have occupied for centuries. Doctors have assumed too quickly—and incorrectly—that they can't influence the course of present-day health care. I have seen no evidence that they have significantly tried to correct our failing system and reassume responsibility for the profession for which they are trained and for which they have sworn to be the guardians. The indifference, bordering on irresponsibility, of today's medical leaders has led to politicians, lawyers, and the media filling their shoes. Unfortunately, these groups often do not have the information, training, and skills needed to make informed decisions or commentaries—but they do it anyway, and all the time, while the leaders remain silent and passive.

Solutions to our health care problems need to originate from a new breed of professional medical leaders, who will need to exercise their leadership role and responsibilities.

Deficient Medical Schools

In 1910, Dr. Abraham Flexner of the Carnegie Foundation for the Advancement of Teaching issued a commissioned report about medical education in the United States. This cornerstone report helped change the face of American medical education by encouraging research, not as an end in itself, but as an aid to patient care and teaching—the first priorities.

Later in the twentieth century, "publish or perish" became the motto in academia. Research became an aim in itself and occupied the foremost importance—at the expense of teaching and patient care. Clinical teaching suffered further when doctors came under increasing pressure to generate more income, while lacking the institutional support, academic recognition, and funding needed to properly perform their job.

In 1985, Harvard Medical School introduced a new MD program, called the "New Pathway in General Medical Education." The program involves a problem-based approach to medical education and promotes interactive, tutorial learning. In response to the changing circumstances of medicine and technological advances, the program encourages students to take responsibility for their own education.

Twenty-one years later, in 2006, courses in medical ethics and professionalism were added at Harvard to the medical students' preclinical years, to ensure continuity in patient experience and faculty monitoring and to engage senior faculty in teaching.[22] The first two years of medical school traditionally offer a structured education in the sciences required for clinical work; ethics is rarely included in the curriculum. These and other modest attempts at reform fill in the gaps created by the evolution of medicine and technological advances. However, they do not address other deficiencies in undergraduate education, like the dropping quality of teaching, underqualified teachers, and the disappearance of the Hippocratic Oath in classrooms and clinics. To claim that a lack of adequate funding is the major reason for these deficiencies is an oversimplification of a more complex problem. Hospital leaders who are fixated on the bottom line do not attempt to be imaginative and inspire doctors to best educate generations of future doctors.

From what I've observed, medical school leaders do not always behave in the impeccable professional manner expected of them, and do not adequately and properly prepare students to work in the medical field. Though they hear about the noble aims of their profession in lecture halls, young doctors are not taught by example how to practice those aims.

What medical students are taught in the classroom may be very different from what is practiced in the real world by their teachers. The

---

22 D. A. Hirsh, B. Ogur, G. E. Thibault, et al., "'Continuity' as an Organizing Principle for Clinical Education Reform," *New England Journal of Medicine* 356, no. 8 (2007): 858.

deficiencies of the medical education system appear in the clinical (the last two) years of medical school, when students rotate in various hospital services and departments, witness clinical care, and even participate in caregiving. For example, Harvard Medical School students rotate among twenty hospitals and health care institutions affiliated with the school. It is no secret that the quality of care varies among these hospitals, and that the caliber of the teaching depends on the interest, expertise, and availability of the professors. Medical students who work in busy practices with a focus on profit are not exposed to good role models; they often witness doctors ordering unnecessary, costly tests, deciding on debatable treatments, and performing questionable surgeries. They also observe doctors making avoidable mistakes and cutting corners, especially when the doctor-patient contact time is absurdly reduced to only several minutes.

Electives and research are encouraged for clinical students who have already chosen a specialization, thus limiting their opportunities to widen their knowledge base. Stress on exciting and promising research, like stem cells and gene therapy, interferes with students' overall clinical education. Since there is no standard clinical curriculum, many students graduate without having acquired the basic knowledge essential for practicing their profession. Medical curricula do not ensure equal attention to all regions of the body. The heart and lungs get, misguidedly, the lion's share of attention. No reforms have attempted to address this obvious deficiency in undergraduate educations.

As a result, I have often observed major gaps in the knowledge and training of the primary care doctors who refer me or with whom I share patients. I have known doctors who cannot perform the necessary evaluations of the ear, nose, or throat of patients—the sites of common infections and allergies. I've even experienced doctor incompetence as a patient myself. For example, I fell once and felt or heard a fracture of one of my foot's bones. The radiologist in the emergency room I went to did not identify a fracture on the X-rays performed. As I was not improving, I consulted an orthopedist four weeks later, who identified an obvious fracture that the radiologist had missed. My complaint to the chief of the radiology department was not taken seriously. The reason I did not sue was personal; I did not want to go through the aggravations. But I had to wonder how a trained radiologist working in a major, Harvard-affiliated hospital could miss an obvious fracture on an X-ray. He could have been too cocky about his skills, fatigued, or simply negligent. I doubt very much that his chief discussed my case with him.

Before I graduated with an MD from the American University of Beirut in 1961, Lebanese law required all the students to spend one year in a rotating internship. I still consider that year to be the most important one in my medical education, because it widened my knowledge base. Unfortunately, the law has since changed, and the rotating internship is no longer required. To save on the number of years needed nowadays for postgraduate training, graduates pick an internship in the field of their interest.

Leaders in medical schools fail to address the important and relevant issues the medical community currently faces. The agendas of the faculty, staff, and committee meetings I attended while working at the Massachusetts Eye and Ear Infirmary and Harvard Medical School usually did not include pressing needs. Issues like quality of care, ethics, medical errors, and the materialism that dominates the practice of medicine are very rarely discussed, to say nothing of resolved, in such meetings. Instead, discussions are limited to the "vital" need to increase income, for example, by milking more money out of HMOs and insurance companies.

Teaching institutions shouldn't assign first priority, as they currently do, to their financial well-being. After Harvard University president Neil Rudenstine announced his resignation in 2001, after a tenure of ten years, Patrick Healy wrote in the *Boston Globe*, "Rudenstine has cemented the cast of today's university president: part fund-raiser, part venture capitalist, part political strategist, and part scholar, when there is time."[23] This is not a reassuring development for the future of college education—and by extension, medical education—in the United States.

Hospitals and teaching centers, obsessed with their bottom lines, have given student education a secondary role; it has become an adjustable tool used to increase income and cut costs. The tuition for medical schools is high (it was $37,200 for the 2006–7 school year at Harvard Medical School), and the federal government gives hospitals tens of thousands of dollars for every resident in training. So, with all of this funding, why are clinical teachers not properly compensated? Tuition and government funds seem to disappear into general budgets, rather than at least partly in professors' paychecks. Universities that expect, and get, free clinical teaching for their students are abusing their power, and have surely realized that the final product—well-educated doctors—undoubtedly suffers from this practice. In fact, since doctors are not remunerated for their teaching,

---

23 Patrick Healy, "He's Leaving Harvard Educated," *Boston Globe*, March 2, 2001.

they often assign it lower priority. For many doctors, the teaching of clinical medicine has become an unprofitable, non-prestigious side activity. This situation must change; the teaching of medical students should be done by dedicated professionals who are well compensated for their time and effort.

In December 2007, Harvard University announced its intention to spend an additional $22 million to assist students from families earning $60,000 to $100,000 per year. It was a pleasant surprise. But according to Steven Ray Goodman, an educational consultant, this decision may not have been an act of philanthropy or civic responsibility, but rather an attempt to avoid losing their tax-exempt status on endowment earnings; this issue was under study by the Senate Finance Committee at the time.[24] In 2006, Harvard spent 4.3 percent of its endowment, which had grown by $5.7 billion; federal law dictates that tax-exempt universities spend at least 5 percent of their endowment funds each year, as private foundations are required to do. Goodman calculates that Harvard saves an estimated $245 million in one year alone by spending only an additional $22 million on student aid. He raised a pertinent question: "Why do American taxpayers continue to subsidize schools that increasingly operate like for-profit companies?"[25]

In a medical school, the highest authority is the dean. Deans vary in how much power they delegate to department chairs, and how much power they decide to exercise themselves. At Harvard Medical School, the dean is geographically separated from the rest of the clinical departments; he is neither easily available nor accessible to faculty members. This setup encourages dictatorial control by the chairs, a control which is never publicly debated or questioned. Any meeting agenda item not approved of by the chair is never seriously discussed, and is usually shelved or written off; criticism, when it rarely happens, is often ignored and rarely mentioned in the minutes.

After deans, chairs of the various clinical departments are next in the line of leaders at medical schools. Before the current explosion in medical knowledge, the chair of a department was the respected authority in his or her field. Currently, the chair has become an administrator, a quality assurer, and, hopefully, an inspirational force in the department.

---

24   Steven Ray Goodman, "The Real Story on Harvard's Generosity," *Boston Globe*, December 31, 2007.

25   Ibid.

Chairs have the ability to hire and fire, determine salaries, and set the climate and priorities of their departments—which everyone follows. They are feared, but not always respected. While at Harvard Medical School, I noticed that chairs' desire and practice of ultimate control was facilitated by the fact that they were independent or semi-independent of the dean, and were located in one of the twenty hospitals affiliated with the university—geographically far from the dean's office. The fact that chairs have open-ended appointments and are usually not seriously reviewed regularly by their superiors encourages such authoritarian control. In order to address this issue, I believe that deans and chairs should undergo regular performance evaluations.

With their status, deans and chairs of medical schools should be able to introduce reform. So why haven't they, when reform has been obviously needed for decades? In my opinion, there are three basic reasons why they do not take action: the complexity of their jobs, the lack of incentives, and the unpleasantness of policing colleagues.

In medical schools, department chairs oversee committees. Committee members and officers are either elected or nominated by the chair. It is not unheard of for a chair to influence a vote by lobbying for his or her candidate before elections. On paper, committees appear to have responsibilities and relative autonomy, but in fact, in order for their decisions to take effect, they need to be approved by chairs or other authorities.

Soon after joining the Massachusetts Eye and Ear Infirmary in 1986, I was appointed to serve on the Joint Operating Room Committee, the most prestigious and sought-after hospital committee. It met monthly to discuss issues related to the operating rooms, the major source of income in the hospital. Discussions were lengthy, and not always serious or relevant. Hospital politics, rather than what really needed to be done, were the basis for a lot of decisions, many of which were never implemented. After several years of serving on this prestigious committee and failing to make a difference with my ideas, I resigned out of frustration. A few months later, I received a letter from the hospital thanking me for my participation in the committee's work and informing me that my appointment had been terminated, instead of acknowledging my resignation. The message was clear: committees are not open to change or criticism.

Often, committees are very eager to legally protect hospitals when mistakes are committed—even when they should acknowledge those mistakes. One morning, I performed sphenoid surgery on a female with chronic headaches, who also suffered from epilepsy. Following the surgery, she recovered from anesthesia normally and regained consciousness. I was very satisfied with her progress when I checked in on her that evening, before going home. About twelve hours after surgery, she went into a status epilepticus (in which the brain is in a state of persistent seizure) and did not recover consciousness, in spite of the appropriate care she was promptly given. She passed away the following day. I suspect to this day that a morphine overdose administered by nurses could have facilitated the events that led to her death, but my opinion was never sought.

A few weeks later, the hospital formed a committee to investigate the cause of my patient's death, and came to the conclusion that no medical errors were committed. Although I was the attending surgeon and the patient was a private patient of mine, I was not informed about the committee formation nor interrogated by any of its members. I consider this lack of follow-through to be egregious; if given the opportunity, I would have brought up the possibility of the morphine overdose. When the Massachusetts Board of Registration in Medicine wrote me, months later, to inquire about the cause of death, I acted responsibly and informed the hospital's counsel and risk manager of my suspicions. It was only then that I learned about the committee just mentioned and the conclusion it had reached clearing the hospital of any wrongdoing. Someone must have known that I was not in full agreement with its conclusion, and had therefore deliberately kept me out of the loop, a clearly unethical behavior.

Business-focused Medical Societies

A large number of professional medical societies in the United States play an important role in teaching and disseminating medical knowledge. Officers of medical societies are elected in a democratic process; they consider themselves accountable to the voters and therefore concentrate on their interests first. Unfortunately, this means that many of the leaders in medical societies do not address the interests and standards of their profession first, but rather appear to be more interested in improving the membership's income. They forget that, as responsible leaders, they are expected to do what is needed for the good of both the public and the profession. None of the societies of which I have been a member have had leaders who have effected positive changes to the practice of my specialty, other than improving doctors' incomes.

The largest medical society in the United States is the American Medical

Association (AMA). Its declared mission is to "promote the art and science of medicine and the betterment of public health,"[26] and its core values include leadership, excellence, integrity, and ethical behavior. The AMA is active in medical education and politics, publishes specialty journals, and involves itself in a variety of projects, ranging from coding and billing to defense of the profession's rights and interests. It has not proven to be the powerhouse that it should be or that its name implies. Surprisingly, the association's activities and track record do not reflect its mission and core values. It lacks a credible reputation for leadership in the medical field; not all U.S. physicians are AMA members. It has not initiated the reform expected to best serve the interests of the general public; instead, it has become part and parcel of the status quo establishment. It has failed to formulate views or actively campaign about such issues as abortion, stem cell research, escalating health care costs, and the millions of uninsured Americans.

Other medical societies have also succumbed to the pressures transforming U.S. medicine from a calling to a pure business. In fact, some societies, like the American Academy of Otolaryngology–Head and Neck Surgery (AAO-HNS) of which I am a member, actually facilitate this transformation. The AAO-HNS is the largest organization of otolaryngologists in the world, with over twelve thousand members. It organizes and sponsors remarkable and impressive teaching programs and activities. It has not done much, however, to preserve the good reputation of the specialty, contain escalating costs, or stress ethical practices. In fact it has contributed to the commercialization of the practice of its specialty. For example, during AAO-HNS's 2000 officer election, the winning candidate ran with the platform of increasing the endowment and forming joint ventures with corporations to build upon the academy's history of education and research. In spite of the candidate's distinguished career and leadership qualities, I voted for his opponent, whose priorities included physicians' autonomy and research funding.

As another example of business priorities, the AAO-HNS's president and chair of the board of governors launched a campaign called "2001: A Sinus-free Odyssey" as part of Sinus Awareness Month in March 2001. The aim of the campaign was mainly profit. Letters to academy members asked them to inform the thirty-seven million sinus sufferers in the U.S. that medical and surgical relief was available for chronic sinusitis, thereby

---

26 http://www.ama-assn.org/ama/pub/about-ama/our-mission.page

indirectly promoting a wave of unnecessary and costly surgeries (see chapter 8 for more on the subject of chronic sinusitis).

Many medical societies have become like unions in recent years, and are fixated on members' benefits. For example, AAO-HNS formed a political action committee (ENT PAC) in order to encourage physicians to participate in the political process. In his letter to solicit contributions from members, the ENT PAC chair outlined three aims of the committee: fight the insurance industry's ability to practice medicine without a license; fight the Health Care Financing Administration's unwarranted activities in doctors' practices; and fight non-physicians who diagnose medical disorders (referring to audiologists who perform hearing tests and prescribe hearing aids, an activity he would like to keep exclusively for ENT doctors). I disagree with the priority given to these actions, because our academy is not first and foremost a union. Present-day audiologists are capable of identifying normal ears, performing hearing tests, and subsequently giving appropriate advice, including hearing-aid prescriptions. I find it odd to witness the Academy wage turf battles, when over the last several decades, ENT has successfully trespassed on the turfs of many other specialties, including allergy-immunology, plastic surgery, oral surgery, and neurosurgery.

A union mentality is often exhibited during the meetings of specialty organizations, which usually occur once or twice a year. At these gatherings, new research is shared; new drugs, equipment, and publications are displayed; and opportunities for socializing abound. These events cater to both the organizations' traditional educational missions, and the financial well-being of the specialty and its members. However, the increasing influence of the pharmaceutical industry on these meetings through generous—though not illegal—grants raises questions of propriety, conflicts of interest, and long-term risks. The missions of medical education and the pharmaceutical industry are not the same, and may be contradictory.

It is not surprising that medical societies have also fallen prey to the growing influence of pharmaceutical companies over their teaching and research activities. In 2007, only 21 percent of the budget of the AAO-HNS came from membership dues.[27] The remainder is provided mainly from corporate support, meetings, and membership fees. I have yet to attend a medical meeting that is not generously funded by pharmaceutical and medical device companies who pay for unnecessarily plush receptions and dinners, and for free seminars run by qualified speakers on their payrolls.

27 AAO-HNS, *Bulletin*, June 2007.

This relationship between pharmaceutical companies and medical societies is too cozy to be risk-free for the future of health care in the United States, and it should be stopped because it is risky and ethically wrong.

Understaffed Teaching Hospitals

Hospital administrators are too powerful. They do not hold themselves accountable to the same standards they set for doctors. They set priorities independently and often ignore doctors' legitimate requests. Unusable tools, broken operating room equipment, and missing supplies are not rare in operating rooms, in spite of repeated complaints. Examination room designs are not always functional, because the doctors who use them are often not consulted during planning. The ease with which administrators add empty threats to ridiculous regulations is remarkable. In one doctors' departmental meeting I attended, a compliance officer was invited to explain new hospital rules regarding billing for services rendered. A Medicare mandate allows a choice between five different levels of billing, with specific conditions that need to be met and documented for each level. Doctors were informed during that meeting that their bills would be regularly audited by hospital compliance officers from that point on, since both under billing and overbilling break federal laws. Noncompliant doctors were henceforth required to take a billing course, at their own expense, and repeat offenders risked losing their hospital admitting privileges. I was the only physician, of the more than twenty hospital-based full-time MEEI and Harvard physicians present, who raised objections about the unjustified strictness of the rules and the impossibility of their implementation. I was ignored. As I expected, these rules, written by bureaucrats, were never implemented. I have also been unsuccessful in swaying hospital presidents who make decisions involving patients without first consulting with their attending doctors. For example, I once had a difficult and argumentative patient who had gone around the country seeking medical opinions on his chronic sinus problems. He then came to me and asked that I perform a certain kind of sinus operation recommended by a colleague in another state. I did not agree to perform that particular procedure and explained to him my reasoning; I also recommended an alternative surgery. He wouldn't take no for an answer and insisted that I perform it. When his dissatisfaction became very apparent, I gave him the names of three colleagues in Boston he could go to. He wound up consulting one of them and had the surgery that I'd recommended, which was different from the surgery the patient had requested and insisted on.

A few months later, the patient wrote me an insulting letter in which he expressed, among other things, his anger at the fact that I billed him for my consultation—even though his insurance paid for my services. I responded with a polite but sarcastic letter that my services and billing were appropriate. Unhappy with my response, he reported me to the president of my hospital, who, without my knowledge or approval, ordered a refund for the patient, since he independently deemed my answer as "not appropriate." I do not know what right a hospital president has to reimburse a patient and overrule instructions to the billing department, without consulting the attending doctor. The patient subsequently reported me to the Board of Registration in Medicine for poor judgment and overbilling. The board acted more responsibly than my hospital's president, and quickly dismissed the complaints as unjustified.

Many hospital chiefs of services do not like it when doctors raise objections to their decisions. In his yearly letter regarding salaries, a chief of ENT tells the doctors in his department, "In the event of a shortfall in revenue or other budgetary or departmental needs, or because of performance or other issues, I reserve, as chief, the right to adjust up or down your compensation (including base salary and incentive compensation), subject to the approval of the compensation committee." Compensation committees never deny chiefs' requests—and doctors have no access to them. The message is very clear.

When the chief of ENT at MEEI offered me a job in 1986, he also wanted me to be the director of one of the five departmental services in need of better organization. He thought my previous administrative experience as the professor and chairman of the ENT department at the American University of Beirut, my alma mater, and my experience as a cabinet member in two Lebanese governments, would be helpful. I accepted the position reluctantly, since I did not want an administrative job and my recent experiences in the eleven years of the Beirut war had drained a lot of my energy.

Several months after I started, I received a letter from the hospital's president informing me that my appointment as a director needed to be renewed yearly, and that I serve at the pleasure of the board of directors. The president did not know that relieving me of the position I didn't want in the first place would be welcomed. I never received an annual letter of reappointment and was expected to stay in that position, and I did, but the message was clear about who the bosses are. I resigned from the job several years later, after I realized that I could not be effective and make a difference in that position. The dictatorial system in that institution was well entrenched and protected. I still wonder why I was pressured to accept a responsibility I did not seek, and then was not provided or allowed the tools to exercise that responsibility.

When patients choose to be treated in a teaching institution, they should be aware of the risks they are sometimes exposed to. Patients and their families are usually not told that residents and fellows often perform some or all of the surgeries, and that attending surgeons are expected to involve trainees in the procedures. Residents spend three to seven years training in the specialty of their choice. If they decide to subspecialize, they must complete one to three more years of a fellowship.

In teaching institutions, the question of who will actually perform a procedure is rarely addressed during the required preoperative consent signing. Oftentimes, when patients ask postoperatively who performed their surgery, they are not told the whole truth. The operative reports meant to reflect and narrate facts tend to underemphasize the role of trainees. This issue needs to be debated openly, so the public knows what is going on in training programs and what needs to be done to train our future doctors.

If patients request that the attending doctor (henceforth referred to as the "attending"), rather than a resident or fellow, perform an operation, the attending becomes morally and legally obligated to comply with the requests. Some of my patients have specifically asked for me to perform their surgery, and I always honored their request. When no preference is stated by the patient, the residents expect to be involved—depending on their skill levels, of course. Trainees need to learn to operate, in spite of the risks involved, and teachers should continue to assume the unavoidable legal and ethical responsibility related to this teaching practice. In some, but not all, surgical operations, the teaching surgeon can closely follow every move made by the trainee, and technical mistakes can be prevented or stopped before damage occurs.

Surgical training programs suffer significantly when residents and fellows aren't allowed to participate actively in surgeries. What would happen to surgical training programs if most patients understood the workings of the health care system, and asked that no trainees be allowed to operate on them? Animals, cadavers, and simulation teaching aids can never adequately replace the experience of performing surgeries on living human beings. By the end of their training, doctors are expected to be skilled, confident, and capable of performing surgical procedures on their own. In other words, they should be experienced. To take the specialty board certification examination, candidates must present a statement to the board outlining how many procedures they have performed and assisted in, before they are certified.

Residency training programs are supported by the federal government, yet hospitals do not hesitate to require residents to perform work with doubtful teaching value. For example, hospitals often place residents, rather than higher-paid emergency room doctors or attendings, in emergency rooms for longer rotations than appropriate. The daily schedules of residents are dictated by the work that needs to be done, rather than by strict educational needs. Resident clinics, which were an important teaching tool for both medical and surgical residents, have disappeared. Currently, training programs rely on the "generosity" of attendings and the policies of teaching hospitals to educate their residents.

Professional regulatory organizations, like the Liaison Committee on Medical Education, the Accreditation Council for Graduate Medical Education, the United States Medical Licensing Examination, and the American Board of Medical Specialties have jumped in to fill in the vacuum of leadership in medical education by instituting strict standards and requirements. For example, as stated previously, an eighty-hour workweek may not be exceeded by trainees, and residents must perform a minimum number of surgical procedures before they take the board examination for their surgical specialty.

Biased Medical Journals

There are over 360 medical journals published in the United States. They are an excellent source of up-to-date information on specialties within the medical field, and influence the thinking and practice of doctors who read them. Though the editors and boards of medical journals have powerful and influential positions, they have failed to consistently exercise their powers well. Every paper submitted for publication is reviewed by peers who recommend or ultimately decide whether or not it should be published.

Because of the peer-review process, readers assume that what is printed in medical journals is scientific, credible, and correct. Unfortunately, with the corporatization of medicine, this assumption is not always justified.

Peer reviewers may not be experts about the subject they are reviewing, and their comments and advice, when negative, are not always relayed to authors in detail. Additionally, impartial expert peer reviewers are becoming rare, because most tend to be on the payroll of pharmaceutical companies; therefore, their objectivity may be appropriately questioned.

Editorial scrutiny often leaves a lot to be desired. A critical look at published material reveals weaknesses that may not be obvious at first glance—and can lead readers to draw incorrect conclusions. There is also the serious issue of conflicts of interest among authors, editors, and publishers—despite disclaimers and preventive rules. Medical journals have not regularly stepped up to the plate to truly address the issues that plague health care.

Unfortunately, repetitious and poor-quality papers are common in today's journals. The prevalent "publish or perish" attitude in academic medicine is partly to blame, because it pressures researchers and academics to publish their research, even if that means doing so prematurely. Ideas are sometimes published before they have been adequately tested or properly researched; these include new surgical techniques that are marketed too early. For a new surgical technique to be practiced, it only needs to have been reported at a professional meeting by its promoter or inventor, and published in a specialty journal. Once it is assigned a code, doctors can bill for it. Not all of these surgical procedures stand the test of time, despite early, misleading reports about their "overwhelming successes."

Since editors are only part-time, it is understandable that they may not have the time or power to ensure the quality of all that is published. Editors are chosen for their professional standing—not their leadership skills—and may be unable to regularly separate worthy submissions from unpublishable ones. Medical editors aren't always vigilant about making sure that all controversial and new ideas are presented as such, and not as definitive solutions that are better than what is already available. When published information proves with time to be incorrect, journals do not always take it upon themselves to correct that false information—information that may still be used by some doctors in good faith.

Medical societies and teaching institutions own most journals, and they either self-publish or contract with publishing firms. Some journals—distributed for free—are owned by publishers or entrepreneurs. These journals are filled with advertisements and have the most lenient acceptance rules for manuscripts. It is doubtful that journals could survive, let alone thrive, without advertisements. Journals may not be legally responsible for the content of the ads they publish, but readers expect editors to have some moral obligation not to publish ads that are misleading or false.[28] The FDA needs to approve new medications before they are advertised and sold. The approval process is tedious, lengthy, and not perfect, but it is the best option available. Advertisers for surgical procedures, tools, or over-the-counter medications do not need to follow this rule. Ad executives in medical journals have sometimes used their power to pressure journals to publish manuscripts that have not passed the peer-review process, to avoid the risk of loss of advertisement income from unhappy patrons.

The *New England Journal of Medicine* (*NEJM*) is one of the most prominent medical journals in the world. It is owned by the much less prominent Massachusetts Medical Society (MMS), which has, for years, financially benefited from the journal without interfering with its operation. Conflict arose in 1999, when MMS decided to exercise its ownership rights and take control of the journal, believing it had been operating too independently. I suspect that it intended to loosen the journal's strict editorial requirements and run it more like a business. As a result, the journal's editor resigned after the takeover. The new editor appointed in 2000 would be expected to listen to and cater to the wishes of the society more than his predecessors did. Soon after his appointment, "the US Food and Drug Administration criticized him for overpraising a new asthma drug made by a company that he had advised as a paid consultant." He admitted his error, but said it was an honest mistake.[29]

Unfortunately, journals have become discreet marketing tools for doctors, drugs, surgical techniques, and devices. Politics play varying roles in medical journals. If an editor is a proponent of an idea or a technique, it is rare to see publications criticize and present opposing or different ideas. There are also articles published in respectable journals that are written by ghostwriters paid by pharmaceutical companies. Such articles prematurely promote new drugs or new indications for drugs. The fact that the authors

---

28 Two advertisements for untested ideas appeared in the academy's annual meeting preview issue in May 2007. One ad was for coblation tonsillectomies, and read "Everything else falls just short." Coblation is a technique that cuts tissue with high-frequency radio waves. There is a claim—still to be tested—that coblation results in less bleeding during and after an operation. The other advertisement was for a nasal spray and claimed that the spray was the most efficient treatment for sinusitis and rhinosinusitis, a misleading, unproven statement.

29 Scott Gottlieb, "FDA Censures NEJM Editor," *British Medical Journal* 320, no. 7249 (June 10, 2000): 1562.

are required to state in their papers that they are paid by companies is not enough to address the conflict-of-interest issue, though it seems to be an acceptable, legally bulletproof argument. At an international meeting of medical journal editors in Philadelphia in May 2001, concern was expressed about when and how research results are made public. Companies have become major funders of research in medicine, and they may delay or never publish results that are unfavorable for them. Editors of major medical journals are pushing to adopt a uniform policy to accept manuscripts for publication, requesting that authors vouch for the integrity of their data.[30]

However, to place all the responsibility for the accuracy of the data, opinions, and conclusions on authors is not right. Editors and reviewers carry a responsibility beyond deciding which manuscripts are worthy of publication. They cannot simply wash their hands of any responsibility regarding what they agree to publish. Professional editors and reviewers should be able to identify or suspect false information in articles. Editors who are too busy with other, non-editing responsibilities to perform this important task should quit if they cannot create time or hire help.

The issue of quality and the bias of some publications remain serious issues. The challenge of quality control in medical journals has become much greater with the increasing popularity of the Internet and digital publishing. Editors and editorial boards need to take a closer and more critical look at manuscripts to ensure the fair treatment of authors and the veracity of published knowledge and opinion, and to keep professional politics, self-promotion, profiteering, and specialty rivalry out.

In 1994, Lucian Leape, a professor of public health at Harvard University, published a criticism of the medical profession in the *Journal of the American Medical Association* (*JAMA*). He chastised the field for ignoring preventable medical errors, long before the Institute of Medicine published its 2001 report.[31] Between 1977 and 2000, the three consecutive editors in chief of the *NEJM* were loud, critical voices of the U.S. health care system. They were critical of for-profit medicine, abuse of managed care, financial conflicts of interest, and political intrusions into medical decisions. The impact of their criticisms—in spite of the editors' influence and the journal's wide circulation and prestige—was never significant.

---

30 Susan Okie, "A Stand for Scientific Independence: Medical Journals Aim to Curtail Drug Companies' Influence," *Washington Post*, August 5, 2001.

31 Lucian Leape, "Error in medicine." *JAMA*, 272:23 (1994): 1851

Leaders in the field, along with practicing doctors and medical professors, do not seem to want to acknowledge or solve these issues. Our system that does not permit the editors of one of the world's most prominent medical journals to impact health care should be reformed.

Arnold Relman, the journal's editor in chief from 1977 to 1991, was harshly criticized by colleagues who did not share his views or observations. He was accused of being arrogant, out of touch, a megalomaniac, a pontificator, an attention seeker, and even a criminal. This last accusation stemmed from his insistence on a rigorous, time-consuming editorial process that was necessary to filter out articles without sufficient merit or that prematurely reported new ideas and findings. His opponents would aggressively argue that the delay in the publication of a paper on a new drug, for example, could have "caused" the deaths of many patients who would have benefited from the drug. He was considered too liberal by the conservative MMS, owner of the *NEJM*. Since the journal is prosperous, in addition to being widely read, Relman was tolerated in spite of his unpopularity among medical doctors.

Jerome Kassirer, editor in chief of the journal from 1991 to 1999, was also critical of U.S. health care. He turned to the *Boston Globe* to express his criticism of what was going on in the medical world. He wrote in a 2001 op-ed, after his departure from the journal, "We have been inconsistent, especially when it came to policing our colleagues and developing enforceable rules for profitable medical activities. We were not tough enough on colleagues who abused controlled substances or alcohol, or those who we knew were practicing substandard medicine."[32] In an address at a 2005 medical gathering, he called for the leadership to be taken back from the "leaders who have allowed the lure of money and the influence of the drug companies to lead them by the nose."[33]

Marcia Angell, the journal's interim editor in chief from 1999 to 2000, crusaded against the troubling business practices of the drug companies and their negative influence on health care. In an editorial published in the *New England Journal of Medicine* in 2000, Angell raised pertinent conflict-of-interest issues that were related to an article in the same issue

---

32 Jerome P. Kassirer, "More Responsible Medical Leadership," *Boston Globe*, February 17, 2001.

33 Jerome P. Kassirer, quoted in *Partners Newsletter* 6, no. 4, April 2005.

reporting on a clinical trial of antidepressants.[34] The authors of that article had more financial ties to manufacturers of psychiatric drugs than the journal space allowed them to list. When this issue was under discussion, Angell encouraged Harvard Medical School to tighten its rules and set an example rather than follow a prevalent materialistic trend and loosen its conflict-of-interest policy. This editorial was quoted on the front page of the *Boston Globe* on the same day that the *NEJM* issue came out. The faculty dean of Harvard Medical School at the time, Dr. Joseph Martin, reacted promptly to Angell's editorial by canceling an imminent faculty meeting during which a decision on whether to loosen the conflict-of-interest policy was going to be voted on. This loosening of regulations was championed by prominent faculty members who had "lent" their expertise to pharmaceutical companies. The dean's fast reaction was an attempt to show how much Harvard worried about conflicts of interest. Yet the policy was later passed quietly, indicating the medical school's unwillingness or inability to prevent conflicts of interest from becoming a fact of life in medicine.

Though leaders in the medical field are to blame for the failures of U.S. health care, they are not alone. Doctors play a part as well. They have to acknowledge this responsibility and do something about it.

---

34 Marcia Angell, "Is Academic Medicine for Sale?" *New England Journal of Medicine* 342, no. 20 (2000): 1516–18.

Chapter Four
Medical Doctors and Their Failings

The majority of medical doctors are competent and ethical professionals who practice their profession as best they can. But the present business climate that has developed around health care has facilitated a serious deterioration of the standards of medical practice. It is true that doctors are victims of the system, but they are also responsible for it in large part, and in many cases perpetuate its deficiencies by their passivity.

First and foremost, doctors have accepted marginalization with no serious objections. For decades, they have failed to acknowledge the writing on the wall, an attitude cynically referred to as "mural dyslexia". Not only have they ignored longstanding, significantly dangerous trends in health care, they have also wrongly assumed they are helpless in its changing panorama. By underestimating their potential power, they have resigned some of their natural responsibilities by failing to intervene and prevent unfavorable events.

Doctors have relinquished their traditional roles as patient advocates and guardians of health. They have allowed themselves to be marginalized in health care matters, reacting passively and self-protectively. In the process, they have lost much of their confidence in their ability to positively influence health care. They've ignored the basic fact that they are health care's main pillars. It is as if they have given up. Indeed, they've clung only to those traditions that serve to protect their self-interests. In that sense, the medical profession's strict code of silence with regard to colleagues' errors, its sensitivity to criticisms from within and without, and its adoption of so-called "political correctness" have all had devastating impacts on quality of care. Second, doctors have embraced, rather than fought, the transformation of medicine into a business. They have ignored major issues surrounding conflicts of interest, assuming wrongly that such conflicts can be contained by writing rules and disclosures—which, instead, create unnecessary monitoring expenses and contribute nothing to patient welfare.

The rise of materialism, the increasing expenses, the decreasing reimbursements, the greedy human nature, and the absence of effective quality and implementation controls have all made it easier for doctors to digest and adjust to the changes, which masquerade as evolution or progress, rather than fight and change them. Doctors are therefore partly responsible for the current, sad state of health care, which is screaming for a timely reform.

The Loss and Subversion of Traditions

It is no secret that modern MDs have metamorphosed into a new breed of professionals who are quite different from the physicians who originally earned the medical profession the reputation and status it once enjoyed. Many doctors have lost their time-honored compassion, becoming cold, powerless providers in a health delivery business.

The Hippocratic Oath

To remind ourselves of the standards to which doctors were once held, let's consider the Hippocratic Oath—and the way in which it has degenerated into a mere ritual. For new physicians, the Hippocratic Oath is supposed to be a defining moment that connects them with centuries of tradition and generations of predecessors, bonds them to all physicians, and reminds them that they should hold themselves to a higher standard than the rest of society, since their role requires higher duties in caring for human suffering. Indeed, holding doctors to a higher standard was taken a step further by the ancient Greeks and Romans, who elevated famous, successful doctors to the level of deities. Similar cultural respect—and expectations—are evident today in the Middle East: in the Arabic language, a doctor is referred to as *hakeem*, which means "wise man."

The power of the Hippocratic Oath, not merely as a symbolic gesture, but as a strong moral and ethical compass, is evidenced by its long history and the durability of its form. The oath dates to the fifth century BC and is attributed to Hippocrates, who practiced and taught on Kos, a Greek island. Hippocrates is generally considered the father of medicine, because he was the first to extricate medical practice from its entwinement with religion and philosophy, giving it an independent status. The oath was originally intended for the group of physicians and healers who followed his teaching, and to distinguish them from quacks and charlatans who were then also practicing the art of healing.

According to its terms, respect and courtesy were owed by doctors to their teachers and their families. Doctors were to be kind to their patients and to abstain from the use of deadly drugs and from performing abortions. The importance of confidentiality was stressed, as was the preservation of the purity of life and the art of medicine. The sick were to be kept from harm and from injustice. Those who did not abide by these principles were not to be allowed into the fraternity of doctors.

For centuries, taking the Hippocratic Oath has been a requirement for all doctors upon graduation, and this tradition has remained universally respected. Additions and modifications have been made over the years to accommodate the thinking of particular medical schools, contemporary circumstances, or cultures. For example, on the assumption that there are no universal moral truths, some universities recently stopped administering the Hippocratic Oath and wrote their own, or even allowed each class to design its own. Nevertheless, the newer versions have largely remained within the spirit of the original, stressing the belief that medicine, both as an art and as a science, is to be practiced with honor and dignity.

Unfortunately, these days the Hippocratic Oath has become an empty ritual. Its philosophical foundations have been undermined, and several of its original intentions have been subverted. Though lip service is still paid to its principles—and indeed, many medical societies use its high-minded principles to shield and disguise their far less high-minded activities—the bottom line is that doctors have lost a crucial part of their education about the traditions of medicine and their ethical code.

The philosophical underpinnings of the Hippocratic Oath have been undermined; patients have become clients, instead of human beings in need of help. In this new world of commercialized care, some philosophers argue that there remain no reasons to hold doctors accountable to any standards higher than those of other businessmen providing other services. Business practices in health care are becoming tolerated and even expected by the public. Art and compassion are no longer stressed or even taught in medical schools, nor are they practiced. They are only "encouraged" in pro forma lectures.

This philosophical stance is inexcusable. True, health care does have a business component, but this is no justification for medical doctors to behave like businessmen, no matter what excuses, instructions, or expectations they and their employers hide behind. Providing health care to individuals, families, and communities is a totally different ballgame than selling a house, a car, a garment, or a meal. The confidence, the comfort, and the support that a medical doctor should provide a sufferer can be as important as the medications and the surgeries available. The requirements of a suffering human being cannot be adequately delivered in a pure business environment.

Defensive Medicine and the Commercialization of Medicine

So far, we've seen how secrecy and "political correctness"—both of which represent a degeneration of the Hippocratic Oath—paralyze doctors and lead to error repetitions. Now let's examine another failure of the medical profession: its continuing, significant contribution to escalating, alarming health care costs.

First, the popular practice of defensive medicine has greatly contributed to the escalating costs of health care. Defensive medicine is the unnecessary or premature use of costly, aggressive means of diagnosis and treatment, especially when worried patients request them. For example, an initial brain MRI is not necessary in all headache cases, but some doctors order them routinely to make sure that they are not missing a brain tumor, a very rare possibility. The widespread abuse of antibiotics in treating upper respiratory symptoms, due to viruses or allergies, is another prominent example of how some doctors practice costly, irrational defensive medicine, sometimes at patients' or families' requests and insistence. The prevalence of defensive medicine has been blamed on the litigious climate of the present days. The threat of litigation has been considered by some doctors as a blanket excuse for practicing defensive medicine routinely. I think that concerns about possible litigations are exaggerated; they do not justify the costs of defensive medicine, and they obscure other, equally important factors motivating doctors in their practice.

Indeed, the true motivators for doctors practicing defensive medicine are more complicated than simple self-protection. For instance, almost no one admits that defensive medicine is popular because it is lucrative to doctors and hospitals. As an example, ENT doctors often perform flexible laryngoscopies on all patients with voice hoarseness or throat complaints, a practice that is not always justifiable, but that allows an extra billing for a "procedure," over and above the billing for the visit.

Defensive medicine is also a result of misinformed or poorly informed public demand—a demand that doctors, unfortunately, have done little to quell. The public feels free to request, not always for good medical reasons, recently advertised, costly "miracle" medications or diagnostic tools. Popular requests include antibiotics to treat nonbacterial illnesses, or a new, expensive PET scan to make sure that a cancer has not spread. Primary care doctors tend to go along with these patient demands without much resistance, as well as with demands for unnecessary, costly consultations with specialists. A cardiac patient insists on having a cardiologist follow up with him, and a diabetic insists that an endocrinologist follow up with her, when actually, their primary care physician may be very competent at handling these two common problems, especially when they are uncomplicated.

Third, defensive medicine is used by some primary care doctors to compensate for inadequate education, training, or skills. They simply pass along cases to specialists that they should be handling themselves. Primary care doctors should learn how to perform adequate ear, nose, and throat examinations; not every patient with impacted ear wax or nasal allergies needs a referral to an ENT specialist. At MEEI, I proposed once that we organize courses to regularly teach primary care doctors how to perform these exams. I was turned down. If we succeed in that project, I was told, we risk getting fewer referrals. Again, business took precedence over cost cutting.

Fourth, doctors use defensive medicine as a timesaving device. Patients may not see the need to make a trip to the doctor, or the doctor may be too busy to see them within a reasonable period of time. A call to the pharmacy to prescribe an antibiotic proves to be a compromise, and everybody is happy. The antibiotic gets the credit for the cure, when true thanks are due to the immune system and to Mother Nature.

To make our discussion of defensive medicine more concrete, let's consider further a prominent example: antibiotic overuse and abuse. Antibiotic abuse illustrates the ways in which doctors' practice of defensive medicine contributes significantly to increasing health care costs, while doing little for patient health. They may even endanger health by encouraging the development of increasingly virulent, resistant bacterial strains and delaying proper diagnoses.

Let me add quickly here my acknowledgement that the introduction of antibiotics has been a major advance in medicine. Antibiotics have helped cure and prevent a large number of infections and have saved many lives. A wide variety of antibiotics are presently available on the market, and newer ones continue to be discovered and manufactured to improve on existing treatments and to attack organisms that are resistant or that have developed resistance to available antibiotics. Unfortunately, there is a public perception that antibiotics need to be used for all infections in order to effect faster cures. In reality, things are not so simple. Respiratory viral infections do not routinely need or respond to antibiotics.

The direct advertising of the pharmaceutical industry to the public, permitted by law, has contributed to this perception. Likewise, the ease with which antibiotics are prescribed, even in doubtful cases, has contributed to the consolidation of this perception. Rather than fighting public misinformation, medical doctors have gone along with it, even to the point of eagerly adopting new, advertised drugs and marketed trends before all the facts are in. That said, I should note for the sake of fairness that some hospital pharmacy committees do impose restrictions on the use of a few new antibiotics because of their toxicity, their tendency to encourage resistance among organisms, or their high price.

In addition to their enthusiasm for antibiotics' powers, many patients and doctors have a false understanding of sinus infections. Earaches, sore throats, and nasal congestion (also referred to, wrongly, as sinus congestion or sinusitis) tend to be considered bacterial infections by many patients and some doctors and nurse practitioners, thus justifying the use of antibiotics, even without the benefit of a physical examination. It is perhaps for this reason that antibiotics are prescribed for 70–80 percent of sinus infections. But this is simply false reasoning; the diagnosis of respiratory infection is often complicated and unclear, as it is widely known that sinus infections are often caused by viruses. And in fact, a recent, widely advertised theory originating at the Mayo Clinic, published widely in the lay press, and reviewed on national TV stated that chronic sinusitis is, after all, a fungal infection, not a bacterial infection. If this theory is proven correct, it may be a good reason for caution in antibiotic use. But, on the other hand, this theory has resulted in a premature increase in the sales of antifungal medications. This just goes to show that doctors and patients have a tendency to adopt newly advertised ideas—which lack quality control—too quickly, before sufficient proof of their truth and efficacy has been established.

To be fair to doctors, fighting patient perception on a case-by-case basis is often a losing battle. For my own part, I occasionally find it difficult to refuse a patient an antibiotic when he or she insists that "I know problems will get worse if I do not take an antibiotic." Arguing with such patients may be time-consuming and futile, because they "know their bodies best." I know certain patients who take an antibiotic daily to prevent the exacerbations of "sinus infections" from which they do not suffer in reality. They claim that when they stop the antibiotics, headaches invariably recur.

In addition to their overuse in treating sinus infections, antibiotics are widely and routinely used in surgery. Yet another prominent example of defensive medicine, this procedure must often be characterized as dubious at best, since supportive and convincing evidence of its efficacy is often lacking. (This is, of course, not to be taken as a universal statement; there are certainly instances in which antibiotics during and after surgery are a must.) In one national meeting I attended, an informal survey of the audience conducted by a presenter revealed that half of the doctors present did not use antibiotics in conjunction with surgery to correct deviations of the nasal septum, while the other half did. The lecturer begged the doctors who don't use antibiotics to publish their experiences more widely, because such reports can make a crucial difference in deciding the outcome of malpractice suits. He had lost such a case in court because he did not use antibiotics on one patient who developed a complication and sued for damages.

Again, to be fair to doctors, fighting public perception on an individual basis is difficult. Indeed, for my own part, I have finally but reluctantly succumbed to the "wisdom" of our legal system, which considers the best medical care that which is "practiced in the community." I now routinely use antibiotics prophylactically on all my nasal operations, against my better judgment. I hope thus to avoid possible patient objections and lawsuits, which I would likely lose.

To sum up, the deterioration of medical care has been aggravated by an insidious process of "liberation" of doctors from demanding and strict professional ethics, traditions, scientific evidence, and expectations. Doctors now tend to be treated as employees in a health-care system that continuously tries to squeeze more work out of them and to compensate them less. So, it's natural to expect them to behave like employees, and it's easy to understand (but certainly not to condone) why self-serving, self-protective, secretive, defensive, and commercial attitudes and practices among doctors have grown and developed, especially among the minority of doctors with weak moral fiber. That said, doctors should take responsibility for having allowed these changes to happen in the first place, and for failing at present to institute user-friendly venues for quality control, self-policing, and reform. Concerned doctors and medical leaders have not shouldered the serious responsibilities of preventing and stopping unethical, risky, and poor practices when they occur.

Chapter Five
Administrators and Regulators

As detailed in previous chapters, the present financial crisis in health care, which is characterized by shrinking resources, increasing costs, and decreasing reimbursements, has resulted in a "mass production" approach to health care. This process has been facilitated by powerful administrators and bureaucrats, who, by complicating the practice of medicine with rules and regulations that are not always justified or reasonable, have thereby increased its costs and decreased its efficiency. They have worked hand in hand to consolidate the transformation of medicine from a noble mission into a business like other businesses, with all the attendant implications and consequences. To be more specific, administrators' and bureaucrats' reliance on unenforceable regulations and complicated billing codes has resulted in arbitrarily high health care costs and invited numerous abuses and injustices.

Hospital administrators have reacted to the problems created by billing codes and other regulations by managing them, rather than solving or improving them. This attitude tends to create new problems that require new management and new levels of bureaucracy, generating vicious circles that are costly and time-consuming. Administrators place increasing income before providing quality care. They actually institute, encourage, and condone unnecessary, controversial, but lucrative treatments, while regarding doctors as machines with only one function, that of generating more money with the least possible expenses. They consider this income-oriented attitude sufficiently justified by the specter of "institutional collapse," a scary, but exaggerated, eventuality nobody wants to risk.

Needless to say, these sorts of actions and attitudes on the part of hospital administrators and regulators have caused considerable dissatisfaction among doctors and patients. In response, regulators and administrators have consolidated their power, so as to protect themselves from backlash. In fact, administrators and regulators have almost completely taken over the control of health care in general and hospitals in particular, although their training is in business and not in human suffering. They have robbed doctors of their roles as patient advocates. As a result, serious patient advocacy has vanished from the present health care system; only its appearance remains. Administrators' power is such that they can even mandate certain medical tests and procedures if they choose to, usually as an attempt to both increase income and avoid lawsuits. Effectively, they practice medicine without a license.

Inevitably, this power and lack of serious accountability have a deleterious effect on administrators' ethics. Regulators are influenced by the very industries they are meant to regulate, while administrators take liberties in breaking regulations if they want to, and in interpreting them as they see fit.

Complicated Codes

Before I go into the ways in which regulators have complicated the practice of medicine, it is worthwhile to define the organizing bodies that publish these regulations. There are two major players in health care regulation. The first is the federal government, represented by Medicare. The other is the Joint Commission on Accreditation of Healthcare Organizations (JCAHO).

As an independent, nonprofit organization, JCAHO's stated mission is to improve the safety and quality of health care through accreditation and related services. JCAHO is truly massive. Since its formation in 1951, it has evaluated and accredited over fifteen thousand health care organizations and programs in the United States. It employs over one thousand people in its surveys force, in order to ensure and evaluate care and compliance with its regulations.

Unfortunately, its governing board has long been dominated by representatives of the industries it is supposed to inspect, and therefore the validity of its evaluations, conclusions, and recommendations must be subjected to questioning. Indeed, I will outline JCAHO recommendations in this chapter that cast serious doubt on this organization's objectivity and priorities.

The other major regulator of health care is the government, and the primary player in this arena is Medicare. Medicare dictates that all medical procedures be reimbursed according to one of five levels of billing codes. It's an incredibly complex system; its 1997 documentation guidelines for evaluation and management of services was fifty-one pages long.[35]

Two other coding systems are needed for billing. The first is the ICD (International Classification of Disease), a World Health Organization (WHO) product. Like Medicare's, the ICD's billing codes are extremely complex. They come in a document over one thousand pages long. It is frequently modified, and therefore contributes to confusion and facilitates mistakes or misinterpretations. In 2005, for example, there were 171 new codes introduced, twenty-five deleted, and 205 revised.[36] The second coding system is the Current Procedural Terminology (CPT) developed by the American Medical Association (AMA) in 1966. It is 708 pages long, and is revised or updated yearly, further adding to the confusion and frustrations.

The Centers for Medicare and Medicaid services (CMS), in their 2004 report, stated that the confusion about which code to pick for services rendered contributed to an estimated overpayment of more than $20 billion to various program participants and an underpayment of $1 billion that stayed in the federal coffers.[37] These reports illustrate the enormity of the problem which has hitherto remained unattended. Just to put this statistic in perspective, $20 billion is only a bit more than the annual GDP of Costa Rica.[38] In other words, American patients are cheated out of enough money each year to sustain an entire *country*!

To illustrate how these regulations affect doctors on the ground, let us again return to the example of the Massachusetts Eye and Ear Infirmary. In an attempt to enforce all of the above codes and guidelines, MEEI adopted in 2006 a "new progressive, corrective policy" to make sure that the documentation used by physicians in their outpatient clinics complied with the government's regulation. According to this new policy, all physicians are audited prospectively on a quarterly basis. When a doctor shows less than

---

35 www.cms.gov/MLNProducts/Downloads/MASTER1.pdf

36 Alice Anne Andress, "Diagnosis coding changes for 2005," *Physician's News Digest*, November 2004, http://www.physiciansnews.com/business/1104andress. html.

37 David Glendinning, "Medicare Zeroes in on E&M Coding as Key Source of Payment Mistakes," amednews.com, January 3, 2005, http://www.ama-assn.org/amednews/2005/01/03/gvl10103.htm.

38 The World Bank, "World Development Indicators (WDI)," WorldBank.org, accessed October 7, 2009.

80 percent accuracy in complying with government coding regulations, he or she is moved to an "occurrence level." Mandatory retraining and reauditing follow. Should there be a second occurrence, education or retraining is mandated. With a third recurrence, further sanctions are taken, including potential termination of employment. Reeducation, if required, is at the expense of the physician.

These unrealistic, bureaucratic rules were never implemented fully, and never will be. In my opinion, they were a costly waste of time, but they look good on paper and protect the administrators.

Why do the current administrators and regulators insist on sticking to and then regularly revising systems that are complicated, costly, confusing, hard to monitor, and easily abused? They should rather work to improve, change, or replace such systems.

Sadly, while codes are a good idea in general, in their present form they are the source of many of the flaws in our current medical system. I'll detail throughout this chapter the abuses and mistakes these codes invite, but for the moment, let me get the bottom line across: these codes are unnecessarily long, ridiculously complicated, constantly changing, difficult to interpret even for compliance officers, and expensive to maintain and monitor. In order to wade through this mess, hospitals need to hire compliance officers to teach and monitor these codes—tasks which are hard, unrewarding, and even impossible sometimes. MEEI, a reputable but relatively small, tertiary-care specialty facility, had a compliance division with a director and three full-time compliance officers while I worked there. That is an expense we could do without! And in addition to maintaining such offices, hospitals must also pay for doctors' continuing education on billing code use.

Medicare and its bureaucrats insist on salvaging the current codes, continually adding to them and modifying them, in spite of the exorbitant cost of their application and failure, and the resultant dissatisfaction and complaints of their users. The decision makers in Medicare have even ignored the advice of government reform panels, which recognized the abysmal failures of these codes. In 2002, the regulatory reform advisory panel of the Department of Health and Human Services recommended that Medicare drop the current coding system altogether, but this advice was never seriously discussed or even acknowledged.

Fake Solutions to Real Problems

Arbitrary billing coding is just the tip of the iceberg in health care delivery; absurd regulations published by JCAHO and government agencies abound. Regulations also cause problems because of the ways in which hospital administrators interpret them, react to them, or elaborate on them. When hospital reimbursement drops, for example, or a new regulation entails a new, costly layer of bureaucracy, more problems inevitably arise. "Managing" these problems, for administrators, does not include addressing the doctors' concerns. It simply means finding ways to recoup lost revenue and cover new expenses. These strategies may include charging an additional "facility fee," taking a bigger cut from the income doctors generate, requiring doctors to see more patients, or pressing lower-paid nurse practitioners, physician assistants, and technicians into service. The unfairness of such measures to hospital staff and patients is never even a talking point. But their impact on quality of care is obvious and undeniable. For example, how can quality care *not* be compromised when one doctor sees thirty or more patients in a three- to four-hour clinic session?

In the following sections, I will detail further how hospitals react passive-aggressively to regulators, and how they take pro forma steps to deal with the subsequent dissatisfaction that regulations cause—in sum, how they "manage" problems rather than actually solve them. Then, later in the chapter, I'll go on to describe how hospital administrators add their *own* complicated, unnecessary regulations as well, with the additional goals of accruing more power and protecting themselves legally.

First, administrators react passive-aggressively to outside regulations, some of which should be actively fought and prevented. As an example of this institutionalized attitude, I can point out that my hospital distributed an instruction booklet to its staff prior to a JCAHO surprise inspection visit planned for 2008. The booklet stated bluntly, "Do not argue with JCAHO surveyors, do not give them more information than they ask for, and do not point fingers or blame others." Indeed, JCAHO has grown and developed to become powerful and more feared than respected. JCAHO surveyors get the treatment of demigods in the institutions they survey. They are rarely questioned.

Why do hospitals react in such a docile manner to JCAHO? The simple answer is that if they don't toe the line, JCAHO has the power to withdraw a hospital's national accreditation, which would entail such dire consequences as the loss of training programs accreditation by specialty boards and possible loss of insurance company coverage of their patients. Therefore, administrators perceive JCAHO's recommendations as orders best left unquestioned.

To be fair to JCAHO, its written standards require that employees who have concerns about the safety or quality of care provided by the hospital may report to it these concerns. But I think this happens infrequently, if at all, because it is not politically correct to do so, and because reporting concerns can easily backfire. This recommendation is more pro forma than genuine.

As a result, one strategy with which administrators "manage" regulations that make little or no sense—or that actually do harm by imposing arbitrary or unnecessary expenses—is to get around the wordings of those regulations. For example, a compliance officer at the hospital I worked in circulated ideas and instructions for making doctors' records compliant with the documentation requirements of Medicare. She stressed it was important to do so in order to avoid hospital citations, which, if repeated, might lead to loss of privileges. She recommended avoiding the words *refer, referred,* and *referral* when documenting a consultation. So, if an attending states his patient was "referred" for an opinion, he cannot bill for a consultation. The record must say the patient was "sent" for an opinion or a consultation instead to justify a consultation bill, which is higher than a bill for a regular visit. This workaround is possible because the term "consultation" has never been clearly defined in manuals. One can easily recognize the temptation to overbill, with a small risk of being caught, because of the impossibility of monitoring every bill from every doctor and health care facility. Some doctors argue that every visit to a specialist is actually a consultation (as it is considered to be in France).

As another example of passive-aggressive resistance to unnecessary and unenforceable regulations, hospitals have failed to consistently comply with a universal protocol issued in 2004 by JCAHO that was designed to solve the serious problem of surgeries conducted on the wrong site, of the wrong procedure, or on the wrong patient. Most of JCAHO's "solutions" to this serious problem have not proved yet to be very effective at eliminating the problem, and hospitals do not always adopt them religiously. For example, the regulation mandates a final "time-out" prior to the start of all surgical procedures in operating rooms, in which all activities stop in the room while a nurse loudly reads the name of the patient, the date of birth, the procedure to be performed, the site of the operation, and the name of the surgeon, to which all the team members must agree before the procedure may start.

But to evaluate this policy, let's step back and consider the steps and procedures that occur before surgery. At MEEI, for example, preoperative patients pass through four different stations, where five different health care staff members ask for and record pertinent information before patients are transferred to the operating room. If a surgeon were going to perform the wrong surgery on the wrong site of the wrong patient after the patient had reached the operating room, then there would be something very wrong with the surgeon and the whole MEEI system. I have not always witnessed the time-out taken seriously, even by the nurse whose role it is to call for it. Indeed, at my hospital, this time-out is sometimes called *after* the operation has started, and sometimes is not called at all. In the same hospital, this rule is not required to be followed or enforced in operations performed under local anesthesia in minor operating suites, confirming my claim that rules are not always necessary. I believe that it is the surgeons' responsibility, and nobody else's, to perform the right procedures on the right patients. Those who are delinquent should be held responsible. It may be time to criminalize irresponsible surgeons' behavior that results in harm.

Naturally, as a result of regulations that have not proved effective, and the poor professional policing practiced, a large number of errors and problems still happen. However, rather than addressing the root source of these problems, including delinquent doctors, administrators again react passively by taking pro forma actions that help them to look good, without actually solving anything. Such measures make the administrators feel protected and comfortable, giving them the false feeling that they have reacted in a responsible manner. For example, the prevailing wisdom among administrators is that manuals that regulate the tiniest aspects of behavior are an effective way to improve health care, to solve medical problems, and prevent fraud and errors. As a result, manuals are often written or revised to "replace" what needs to be done to enforce real accountability, education, training, and serious monitoring. One hospital, for example, responded with ridiculous paperwork when a mistake that resulted in a fatality was publicized. An accident victim was brought in with neck injuries. The supervising nurse failed to consider the possibility of a cervical spine fracture, and therefore the neck was not immobilized. The patient developed paralysis in all four limbs and subsequently died, although her other serious injuries contributed to causing the fatality. The subsequent investigation concluded that the emergency department staff was unfamiliar with cervical spine trauma, and so a procedure manual on how to handle cervical spine injuries in the emergency room was prepared. The possibilities that the nurse was not well trained, was overworked, or was fatigued because she worked two jobs to pay her bills were not even considered. The hospital ended up with an extra manual that collects dust alongside all the other manuals that not many people ever read or remember.

In addition to writing manuals, hospital administrators like to add rules of their own to the already compendious rules imposed by external regulators. Many of these rules reflect administrators' desire to protect themselves legally from malpractice suits, and are simply a waste of time. For example, when patients arrive at one hospital for a surgical intervention, they are asked six times by six different people if they are allergic to any medications, and the answer is recorded ten times, not six, in different places of the medical records, and sometimes more than once on the same page. In an emergency room record, the doctor writes down the medications and the instructions given to the patient. On the *same* page of the record, the nurse rewrites exactly the same information. This is a waste of time. I asked a nurse once about the wisdom of this silly, time-consuming routine. She responded, without conviction, that it was to ensure that the patient understood all the doctor's instructions. But if this reasoning were justified, a nurse's note would need to follow every doctor's note with instructions in all medical records! I have witnessed preventable medical mistakes happen because the doctor who wrote the prescription orders didn't want to bother or lacked the time to go over a lengthy medical record. For example, I witnessed a doctor order a medication to which the patient was allergic, because he didn't want to look at a record that listed allergies to drugs several times. Quality care is not helped by administrators or nurses who like to trespass on doctors' responsibilities, which should include timely self-policing. This latter idea is one of the aims and propositions of this book.

I can only imagine the lengthy meetings and the number of drafts prepared and discussed before the above rule was approved by a group of administrators and their staff, who did not perceive that there was other, more important work to do. Regulations written in response to errors end up penalizing all doctors, rather than rightfully targeting offenders. They therefore waste time and add paperwork.

Far worse than simply wasting time and penalizing all doctors for mistakes and omissions committed by a small minority, manuals and regulations fail to address the serious, underlying causes of problems, such as the lack of appropriate education and training for many residents, and the serious lack of adequate staffing at many hospitals. In particular, staffing shortages extend from the lowest ranks to the highest. For example, at my hospital, there are fewer telephone operators than necessary. As a result, phone calls are not always answered in a timely manner, even during evenings and nights, when the pressure of work is usually low. Likewise, some offices are severely understaffed when it comes to secretaries. As a result, patients' messages to their doctors are not delivered and calls are not returned. Some telephone lines remain busy for hours. I know of secretaries who have the habit of taking their telephones off the hook when they are too busy to answer. I have not witnessed administrators tackle these issues seriously, except by banning this practice without looking into what caused it. Additionally, it is not easy to monitor such a ban.

At a higher level, the understaffing of supervising doctors and anesthesiologists in teaching hospitals may result in preventable medical errors. In my experience, emergency rooms are often manned at night and on weekends by unsupervised junior residents, consequently lowering the quality of care and increasing the risk of medical errors. At MEEI, the absence of an anesthesiologist on the premises during nights, weekends, and holidays, and the unwise assignment of patients with serious acute respiratory problems to available but inexperienced ENT residents heightens the risk of serious errors, injuries, and even death. The argument that an anesthesiologist is rarely needed at night for respiratory emergencies is not a good enough reason to risk such substandard care in a reputed, Harvard-affiliated hospital. To be fair, such practices are far from unique to MEEI. In fact, the nationwide prevalence of substandard care in emergency rooms is known, and has been unfortunately accepted by society as a fact of life.

In sum, hospital administrators react to problems by passively accepting outside regulators' external pressures. Displaying poor leadership, they issue countless regulations and manuals that shift the responsibility for mistakes to hospital staff, while ignoring root causes. Such half measures are unlikely to protect hospitals in court, and fail to address major, urgent issues in health care, like the need to adequately train residents and employ sufficient numbers of staff.

Predatory Billing

Unfortunately, hospital administrators do far worse disservices to the practice of medicine than simply misspending money on frills like ads and consultants or investing in useless manuals and doubtful, untested tests and procedures. To put it simply, they not only fail to control rising health care costs, but at times actually *encourage* those rising costs. In my long years of practice and teaching in Boston, I have participated in numerous meetings and witnessed serious, ongoing efforts to increase income, but never efforts to cut costs. Such income-generating efforts take the form of encouraging overbilling through overdocumentation, manipulating resources so as to make care expensive for the patient, and even engaging in billing practices reminiscent of loan sharks' tactics. Indeed, the settlements recovered by the Justice Department in fraud cases, mostly against hospitals and health care providers, amounted to $3.1 billion in 2006.[39]

First, hospital administrators do not merely accept the unnecessarily complicated billing codes described above and designed by external regulators; they actually encourage their abuse, and thus greatly contribute to the sharp rise of health care costs. Hospital administrators primarily encourage such abuse by demanding overdocumentation and redundant, unnecessary services.

Power Corrupts

I've outlined how hospital administrators react passively to regulators, while always seeking to increase their income and promote their image, often through pro forma steps. However, as one might imagine, they've also taken steps to consolidate their own power, in order to protect themselves from the dissatisfaction they face as a result of the regulations they institute and the unorthodox, income-seeking measures they take. In particular, they have stolen the role of patient advocate from doctors. Administrators exert power by arbitrarily insisting on enforcing certain regulations if it suits their purposes, while flagrantly breaking and ignoring others.

In conclusion, the power that regulators and administrators enjoy has reduced the quality of health care, marginalized the pillars of medicine

---

39   *Time*, "Numbers: Dec. 4, 2006," November 26, 2006, http://www.time.com/time/magazine/article/
0,9171,1562934,00.html.

(doctors), and driven up costs. Regulating bodies such as JCAHO and Medicare have imposed complicated, arbitrary billing codes that invite abuse, while administrators have reacted passively to such regulations. Administrators engage in image-building and often take pro forma steps to manage problems rather than solve them. Even worse, administrators actively increase costs by encouraging overdocumentation, redundant services, and predatory billing practices. Many of these behaviors and circumstances have been made possible because regulators and administrators have very little accountability. They have thus been able to consolidate power and then defend it in the face of dissatisfied patients and doctors, while robbing doctors of their important roles as patient advocates. Their obsession with increasing income and their focus on competition and growth need to be critically reevaluated.

Of course, I don't want to give the impression that hospital administrators and regulators are the only "villains"; the book is candid about exposing all others at fault. They do face outside pressures, not the least of which are those imposed by insurers and special interest groups. Unfortunately, their reactions to such pressures have been ineffective at best. In fact, a parallel can be drawn between the ways in which doctors passively allowed outside forces to usurp and debase their roles, traditions, and values (a process that I detailed in chapter 4) and the ways in which health care regulators and hospital administrators have not been active enough in fighting trends that threaten their ability to provide affordable quality care.

Chapter Six
Insurance Companies

Insurance companies are major players in our health care system; indeed, care delivery is built around them. As a result, insurance companies have become major contributors to high health care costs. Insurers' generosity to politicians has allowed them to exercise more power in Congress than is compatible with good and responsible health care. In effect, they remain unaccountable; they decide on eligibility and benefits, deductibles, the timing and amount of payments, and other issues in which they have a financial concern. All this power comes at the detriment of the patient in particular and health care in general. The fact that these companies—and their executives—are very prosperous, while the system is close to bankruptcy, shows just how anomalous and unacceptable the situation has become.

As a result, the inadequacy of insurance coverage in America is now nothing short of dire. In 2006, forty-six million Americans, or 15 percent of the population, had no insurance coverage, a few million more than in 2007.[40] The percentage of working-age Americans with moderate to middle incomes who lacked health insurance for at least part of the year rose to 41 percent in 2005, a dramatic increase from 28 percent in 2001.[41] In 2005, 39 percent of employers offered no medical benefits, up from 31 percent in 2000, and about 60 percent of employers stated they expected medical

---

40   U.S. Bureau of the Census, *Income, Poverty and Health Insurance Coverage in the United States: 2007,* August 2008.

41   Theresa Agovino, "More People with Moderate and Middle Incomes Lack Health Insurance, Study Shows," Associated Press, April 26, 2006.

coverage to decrease.[42] This lack of coverage has resulted in very real, tragic consequences: according to a 2004 Institute of Medicine report, eighteen thousand adults die unnecessarily each year because they lack coverage.[43]

Meanwhile, even individuals who have insurance do not necessarily always get the care they need; insurance companies often fail to deliver on their promises. In fact, insurance companies seem to make their coverage and billing policies deliberately complicated in order to obscure the extent—or rather, the inadequacy—of care they provide. Thus, consumers are put in the unique position of buying policies without knowing exactly what they cover. In other words, the policies insurers issue for their clients are so complicated, so lengthy, and so full of small print, that even highly educated people cannot understand them—when they decide to read them (which seems to happen only rarely). Worse still, these policies may change suddenly, in the middle of a billing term. If patients call to ask questions, they get noncommittal and sometimes-contradictory answers to the same questions related to coverage, from phone operators or clerks who often appear to know very little. The absence of responsible medical leaders facilitates the trespassing of the insurance companies.

Likewise, insurers' billing procedures with regard to in-network and out-of-network coverage are often so complicated as to be nonsensical. As an example, a patient of mine once asked me about the total cost of the surgical procedure I proposed for her. I referred this question to the appropriate sources in the hospital, and this is the answer I received: "Dr. Salman is in network and will be covered 80 percent. The patient has a $400 deductible. However, the facility, MEEI, is out of network. The insurance will only cover 40 percent and the patient will be responsible for 60 percent of the rest." Try to figure that out. Such complicated rules make it next to impossible for patients to check on possible mistakes in bills. I suspect they were created to intimidate patients and doctors, and to discourage them from trying to understand and therefore being able to ask questions and argue.

Such complicated rules lower patient care on two fronts: they confuse patients, and they confuse doctors as well. When doctors have to waste their time trying to figure out regulations, they sacrifice time they could

---

42 Kathleen Kingsbury, "Pressure on Your Health Benefits," *Time*, October 29, 2006, http://www.time.com/
time/magazine/article/0,9171,1552040,00.html.

43 Madeline Drexler, "Curing Our Public Health System," *Boston Globe*, February 11, 2006.

be spending with patients. Indeed, insurers put the burden of filling out paperwork and understanding policies on doctors. For example, in 2006, Blue Cross and Blue Shield of Massachusetts (BCBSMA) distributed to physicians a document labeled as a "non-covered drug conversion tool." When a doctor wants to prescribe an uncovered drug, comparable covered drugs are listed in this conversion table to help him or her choose a covered alternative. This list represents an additional, unreasonable burden; it is unrealistic to expect busy doctors to remember which company covers which medications. Moreover, the fact that this list might change at any time serves to confuse doctors further. Why should the burden of choosing covered alternative medications rest with the doctor? There must be better ways to address this issue.

The billing issue becomes even more confusing when one considers the fact that insurers' coverage policies differ. For example, some insurers, including Medicare, follow a "global surgical billing practice." Their coverage of a surgical procedure covers the pre-op visit and ninety days of post-op care. But other insurers do not follow this policy, so the surgeon must remember which companies do or do not provide coverage for postoperative care before submitting a bill. Such tasks constitute an extra, time-consuming chore for the busy doctor and office staff, and come at the expense of the time allocated to the patient.

Such complicated and changing policies often hide very real deficits in the insurance companies' offerings; they even hide corrupt selling procedures. For example, employers are usually offered many insurance options for their employees. Brokers are called in to help choose the best option for each employer. For their services, the brokers are usually paid 2–8 percent of the deal, drawn from the employers' premiums. Employers are usually not aware of this "incentive" offered to brokers. Apparently there are no laws against this practice, so it is not really illegal, yet is it right or ethical? "Plans usually build commissions into the premium rate charged to firms regardless of whether a firm used a broker."[44] In 2003, BCBSMA paid $66 million in broker commissions. This included $14 million in bonuses. Brokers defend this practice by stating that the bonuses are too small to influence decisions and that all insurance companies offer

---

44 Leslie Jackson Conwell, "The Role of Health Insurance Brokers: Providing Small Employers with a Helping Hand," Center for Studying Health System Change, October 2002, http://www.hschange.com/CONTENT /480/480.pdf.

them[45]—but such large sums seem to render this claim obviously false, and contribute to rising health care costs.

As a second example, health plans often advertise deceptive lists of physicians available to their subscribers. Such lists include the names of doctors who have moved or died, who do not accept new patients, or who are willing to see new patients only after several months of waiting. These lists have been referred to as "phantom networks." On paper, everything seems to be fine, as a large number of primary care physicians and specialists are supposedly available. But when a subscriber tries to get an appointment with one of them, these phantom networks become obvious, and the frustration of trying to get an appointment with an appropriate doctor begins.

When needed health care services are denied or delayed, patients and doctors have the option of appealing insurers' decisions—but this process is time-consuming and user-unfriendly, and the odds are unfairly stacked in favor of the insurer. Responses to appeals are decided upon behind closed doors and mailed to patients and their doctors, sometimes without a signature or the name of a person to contact or respond to. In such appeals, insurance companies are actually both the adversaries and the judges—a patently unfair and unjust situation.

The result of such denied services and appeals has been numerous lawsuits filed against insurance companies over the years. To take an example, class-action lawsuits have been filed by the American Medical Association and several state medical associations against the largest insurance companies in the U.S., Aetna Health and CIGNA, on behalf of physicians who charged that their patients' insurance companies had conspired to curb reimbursement for physicians' services. The plaintiffs represented eight hundred thousand physicians who had treated patients enrolled by the defendants during the previous decade. These companies had to pay $50 million in settlement and promise to create a new, better database.[46]

Blue Cross

So far, I've spoken of "American insurance companies" without going into much detail about specific companies. But to be more concrete, let's

---

45   Liz Kowalczyk and Andrew Caffrey, "AG Probes State Health Insurers," *Boston Globe*, November 14, 2004.

46   Molly Merrill, "AMA, Others Join Lawsuits against Aetna, Cigna," HealthcareITNews.com, February 10, 2009, http://www.healthcareitnews.com/news/ama-others-join-lawsuits-against-aetna-cigna.

further examine one insurance company, as an example of the sorts of problems that occur on a larger scale. The Blue Cross and Blue Shield Association (BCBSA) is a nationwide federation of thirty-nine health insurance organizations and companies that directly or indirectly provide insurance to over one hundred million Americans, or, in other words, to around one-third of the country's population. I'll focus on one of its regional companies, Blue Cross Blue Shield of Massachusetts (BCBSMA). BCBSMA is the biggest insurer in the state of Massachusetts, and covers over 3 million people, out of a population of 6.5 million. It has continued to enjoy its nonprofit status since it was established in 1957 with a mission "to make affordable healthcare available to the people of Massachusetts."[47] Unfortunately, it has engaged in essentially face-saving activities—more political than practical and significant—to help justify its nonprofit status and the significant tax advantages it continues to enjoy. BCBSMA created a charitable organization in 2001, the Blue Cross Blue Shield of Massachusetts Foundation. Endowed with $55 million, the foundation was meant to be a contemporary expression of "historic commitment to those in need" by enhancing services to the uninsured.[48] But in 2004, this foundation gave a paltry $2.5 million in grants, less than the salary and benefits of its CEO.

Meanwhile, in 2004, 7–10.5 percent of the Massachusetts population remained uninsured.[49] Since the passage of the new health care law in Massachusetts, in 2006, coverage has become close to, but not totally, universal. But the premiums have increased and are projected to double by 2020.

As lawsuits have demonstrated, BCBSA organizations nationwide have not lived up to similar promises. In 2003, a national class action suit was filed by nine hundred thousand physicians against the vast majority of the BCBSA health plans in the country. The complaint was that these companies had schemed to defraud doctors and improperly deny, delay, and reduce payments. A settlement was reached in 2007, four years later, in which the defendants agreed to improve their business practices, commit to better communication with doctors, and establish an independent external

---

47   Blue Cross Blue Shield of Massachusetts, "Our History," https://www.bluecrossma.com/visitor/about-us/our-history.html.

48   http://bluecrossfoundation.org/~/media/Files/Policy/Roadmap%20to%20Coverage/020101RTCLifeOnTheEdgeWiclawski.pdf

49   Theresa Agovino, "More People," NetscapeNews.com, April 26, 2006.

review board for resolving disputes. They also agreed to pay $128 million to class members.[50] This settlement was of historic importance because of its size and because of the clout of the Blues.

But in spite of such nationwide lawsuits against its parent organization, BCBSMA—a nonprofit organization, remember—seems to continue to be very profitable. For example, BCBSMA continues to pay its board members (which is unusual in the nonprofit world), and moreover, it pays them quite handsomely. The chairman, president, and CEO of BCBSMA received $3 million in 2001 and $3.2 million in 2002. In contrast, the president and CEO of Harvard Pilgrim Health Care received only $562,000 in 2001 and $807,000 in 2002.[51] BCBSMA also paid its former chairman and chief executive William C. Van Faasen a $16.4 million lump-sum retirement benefit.[52]

Such profitability is part of a larger pattern: nationwide, insurers continue to make enormous sums and pay their executives high salaries; even as hospitals go bankrupt, the number of uninsured grows, benefits drop, and co-pays increase. When compared to the insurance systems of other countries, the inefficiencies of this situation become obvious. For example, a 2003 study published by the *New England Journal of Medicine* found that the average overhead of U.S. insurance companies is 11.7 percent, compared to 3.6 percent for Medicare and 1.3 percent for Canada's National Health insurance (which is government-run).[53] That "overhead" represents salaries of executives and administrators, and is both detrimental to health care and completely unjustifiable. The lesson is clear: private insurance companies are costly, so why not embrace the so-called public option?

Why do BCBSMA and other insurance companies get away with this sort of behavior? One reason must be that they gain protection for themselves through political contributions and lobbying. For example, BCBSMA

---

50 Kaiser Health News, "Blue Cross Blue Shield Association Settles Class-Action Lawsuit Filed by 900,000 Physicians," April 30, 2007, http://www.kaiserhealthnews. org/daily-reports/2007/april/30/dr00044580.aspx ?referrer=search.

51 Jennifer Heldt Powell, "Blues' CEO Earned $3M-Plus," *Boston Herald*, November 15, 2003.

52 Robert Weisman, "State Targets Health Care Officials' Pay," *Boston Globe*, September 3, 2009.

53 Michael Hochman and Steffie Woolhandler, "Healthy Skepticism," *Boston Globe*, October 28, 2006.

donated $1 million to the 2004 Democratic National Convention held in Boston. Why? For political influence, obviously. It seems obvious that funds that went to politicians could have been used more appropriately to lower insurance rates and increase affordability and coverage.

Insurers Practice Medicine

As a consequence of the lack of accountability that insurance companies have "bought" for themselves through political influence, they've been able to act almost unilaterally in regard to coverage. Like the medical administrators described in chapter 5, insurance companies, in effect, cut costs by practicing medicine without a license, making health decisions that should belong only to the medical profession. They write and change policies, reduce payments, and increase co-payments. They do all of this at their convenience, frequently in the middle of a contract, and irrespective of their previous agreements and of their impact on their patrons in particular and on the public health in general.

First, insurance companies claim to be "experts" in health care in order to justify decisions that are detrimental to patients both in terms of delivery and in terms of actual care. For example, in terms of health care delivery, one insurer announced it would levy higher co-pays for health care providers that had a history of higher costs and lower efficiency.[54] But that raises the question of whether insurance companies have the expertise to judge the "efficiency" of hospitals. Indeed, how can these attributes be determined accurately and fairly, across the spectrum of medical specialties? The author doubts the success of the outcome studies, even when conducted by the medical profession, in fairly addressing this issue.

Furthermore, insurers claim that their "expertise" allows them to judge not only the delivery, but also the substance of health care. More particularly, they question, dictate, and alter doctors' prescription decisions. For example, in 2006, Tufts Health Plan in Massachusetts cut a patient's prescription for the sleeping pill Lunesta from thirty to ten pills per month.[55] This decision was based on the judgment of the company's prescribing

54 Jeffrey Krasner, "Blue Cross Plans to Rank Providers," *Boston Globe*, August 19, 2006.

55 Christopher Rowland, "Fed-up Doctor Sidesteps Insurance Company Limits," *Boston Sunday Globe*, June 11, 2006.

committee, which determined that most patients take this medication on an occasional basis, and would therefore not need more than ten pills per month. Who are the members of this company's prescribing committee, and who are they accountable to, other than the company that employs them? This decision was certainly based on financial reasoning, rather than on sound medical judgment.

As another, personal, example, I once prescribed Allegra, an antihistamine for nasal allergies, to one of my patients. Soon after, I got a letter from Medco, the company that managed the prescription drug benefit for my patient, on behalf of his plan sponsor. The letter asked me whether I had tried another antihistamine, Loratadine, or any other over-the-counter prescriptions, and whether or not these had failed to treat the patient's condition. I'd chosen that particular drug based on the patient's personal history, a choice which to me seemed an inherent duty—and prerogative—of a physician. Indeed, as would seem obvious, there are a variety of reasons for choosing a particular medication. For example, although antihistamines are supposed to be similar in action, they may have different effects on different people. Some patients respond best to specific ones. Other patients may request specific prescriptions because their over-the-counter equivalents are not covered by insurance—and why not, since money is the name of the game everybody else plays? Questioning such physician decisions, therefore, is both presumptuous and clumsy.

To be fair, I understand that insurers question physicians in an effort to cut costs that sometimes represent valid concerns and problems. But insurance companies' efforts to solve such concerns are so inept as to be useless, or even harmful. For example, insurance companies have tried to address the serious, widespread, and chronic problem of nasal septal surgeries performed without proper indications. However, they've done so in a completely ridiculous way. To again cite personal experience, a thirty-year-old truck driver once came to see me with a ten-year history of bilateral nasal blockage, snoring, sleep apnea, and sleepiness while driving. He had fractured his nose playing football in the past. When I examined him, I found a severe deviation of his nasal septum which blocked the airways on both sides. I recommended an operation to fix the deviation to improve his nasal breathing and hopefully his snoring. He was scheduled to have the necessary surgery.

One business day before the surgery, my office was informed that his insurance company had refused to certify the surgery. They stated that they needed to know the percentage by which the deviation obstructed the space between the inferior turbinates and the septum. In other words, if the patient's blockage were greater than 75 percent, the surgery would be approved, but if it were only 50 to 75 percent, they would not approve the surgery until the patient had first been treated with medications that failed to bring him any relief. There is no reference in the medical literature to support this arbitrary and silly decision. The surgery was inconveniently cancelled one day before it was scheduled to take place.

The following week, I received a letter signed by an MD, informing me that the patient had *not* already undergone and failed medical treatment, so the surgery couldn't be justified and approved. I responded with a rhetorical question: could he recommend drugs that address traumatic septal deviations? A week later, I received a letter from the same doctor informing me that "my request for reconsideration" (a request that I never submitted) was approved. I've also received letters in other cases for similarly silly reasons; once, a sinus CT scan was denied for one of my patients because "he has not been on antibiotics, nasal decongestants, or nasal steroids for at least four weeks." What a nonsensical, arbitrary, across-the-board requirement! And what a waste of bureaucrats' and my time, at the expense of patients' well-being.

Such clumsiness is hardly confined to my personal experience; most doctors have dealt with it. The BCBSMA medical policy manual has listed uvulopalatopharyngoplasty (UPPP) as a treatment for obstructive sleep apnea and upper airway resistance syndrome (UARS). It has recommended, however, that prior to a UPPP, these conditions should be treated with a continuous positive air pressure (CPAP) device and with weight loss, if indicated. These recommendations, in practice, have become unfair requirements. Some patients cannot tolerate CPAPs or refuse categorically to use them, and weight loss is often difficult or impossible to achieve. More to the point, the province of such decisions should rest with medical leaders and experts, not with insurers.

Often, insurance companies go a step further than clumsy interventions; they practice medicine without even bothering to claim that they are experts or that their cost-cutting concerns are valid. At such times, their policies are transparently designed to reduce services to patients, and are completely arbitrary in terms of logic. These actions have two effects: they reduce the amount of care patients receive, and they actually change the way doctors perform procedures.

First, changes in coverage usually reduce the availability of appropriate care. For example, in 2006, BCBSMA opted to cover the relatively new PET/CT scans for many cancer patients, but not for breast cancer patients.[56] To explain, the PET/CT scanner combines two types of radiological scans in one, and is a highly accurate diagnostic tool. It has been successfully used to track the spread of malignant cells in the body and to evaluate the extent of damaged heart tissues in heart attack patients. It has also been used to monitor epilepsy and Alzheimer's disease. Since breast cancer patients are treated more often than many other types of cancer patients and are extremely likely to benefit from a PET/CT scan, BCBSMA's decision could not have represented anything but financial self-interest. It made a discriminatory medical decision that did not fall under its proper scope of responsibility and got away with it. Fortunately, to the best of my knowledge other insurers did not follow suit.

Second, arbitrary coverage can actually affect how doctors perform their tasks. For example, if two or more surgical procedures are performed at the same time, insurers may pay solely for one of the procedures of their choice, usually the less costly one. They refer to this practice as bundling. So, in response, surgeons separate or space out their surgical procedures. I know of a sinus surgeon who once performed bilateral sinus surgeries on a patient one side at a time, rather than on both sides at the same sitting. In this way, he was paid more than he would have been paid had he operated on both sites at the same time (as is usual). The patient ends up being the loser in such a situation, because of the unnecessarily increased risks of a second surgical procedure and the lengthier morbidity time. To make the bundling practice even more unfair, hospital administrators kept doctors in the dark about these policies and practices, in spite of doctors' requests to learn about their details. The fraternity between hospital administrators and insurance companies has taken priority over the interests of doctors and over what is fair or right.

The Passive Medical Profession

Why have insurance companies gotten away with unilaterally determining coverable hospital stays, procedures, and medications? I've already pointed to insurers' political clout—but at the same time, the medical profession must bear some of the blame. At the ground level, at

---

56 Christopher Rowland, "State OK's Medical Scanners, Renews Cost Debate," *Boston Globe*, April 19, 2006.

the leadership level, and at the administrative level, medical professionals have failed to fight the unfair transgressions of powerful insurance companies.

First, at the ground level, physicians have allowed insurance companies to trespass, dominate, and enforce decisions by reacting passively to their mandates (for more on such passivity, see chapter 4). Doctors have not complained forcefully or resisted effectively, but have instead expressed pro forma or off-the-record objections here and there. Instead of speaking out to solve issues or disputes, they are more likely to accept the rules and then bend them to protect their interests and those of patients in order to save themselves time and aggravation. After all, for doctors to get actively involved and fight the insurance industry is frustrating and time-consuming—and time is money. So instead, they turn the other cheek, while seeking ways to bend the rules.

Second, it is unfortunate that medical leaders and professional societies have behaved in a similar manner to physicians. As an example of this sort of passivity, in 2004, the Massachusetts Medical Society made an unsuccessful and tardy effort to prevent Harvard Pilgrim Health Care (HPHC), a Massachusetts HMO, from cutting imaging services. HPHC, in association with the National Imaging Associates (NIA), established a program to require preapproval before orders for costly diagnostic imaging services, like CT scans and MRIs, were carried out.

HPHC's efforts were, in effect, an effort to optimize the use of imaging and to cut costs, which is a valid concern—but it went too far. The overuse of expensive imaging studies by doctors is a common and well-known problem. However, since that is the case, the Massachusetts Medical Society (MMS) should have proposed a plan to tackle this important issue long before Harvard Pilgrim trespassed on the provinces of the medical profession. Indeed, the very fact that the insurers took action shows how passive medical societies in general have been in trying to control costs.

Instead, MMS only responded to this important health care cost issue when the insurers took action; they announced their objection in a newsletter to their members because of "the impact this program [would] have on the physician's relationships with their patients, and the serious effect the policy [would] have on the management of practices and the morale." (The author disagrees with this reasoning, as there are better reasons than these to object to this decision.) MMS representatives subsequently met with the insurance officials behind this decision and proposed a moratorium on the ruling, which was denied, as expected.

MMS also proposed the immediate creation of a task force to enforce appropriate use of costly imaging studies. In a letter to its members in August 2004, MMS explained that it had strongly articulated its concerns, met with HPHC leaders, and created a task force on medical cost control, in order to implement evidence-based clinical guidelines for the entire Massachusetts health care system. As of February 2007, unsurprisingly, I had not received any guidelines. No such task force was ever created, and the insurer prevailed. The medical society's actions were too little, too late, and simply pro forma.

Third, hospital administrators act passively in response to insurers' decisions. Rather than trying to address the known and common abuse of costly diagnostic studies and working to change policies that favor the financial interests of insurance companies over patients' well-being, hospitals play games with insurance companies. For example, instead of arguing over coverage changes, hospitals modify their logistics in order to adapt to new requirements, so as to avoid losing revenue. A widespread example of this sort of behavior is the creation of a "twenty-three-hour observation period," a new class of hospital stay. I'll go into detail with this example, because it tellingly illustrates the ridiculous nature of these games, which are costly and time-consuming to design, teach, apply, and monitor.

The twenty-three-hour admission, or "observation" period, was created in response to insurance companies' decisions to reduce their coverage of surgical procedures that entail a stay in a hospital. Instead, insurers elected to cover certain procedures only when performed on an ambulatory basis. Such decision making is tantamount to practicing medicine without the needed credentials, license, or accountability. As an example of such reductions in coverage, BCBSMA announced once in the middle of the year in the late eighties that it would stop covering the expenses of a tonsillectomy if the patient were admitted to a hospital. It would provide coverage only if the surgery were performed on an outpatient basis. This was an all-or-nothing policy; if the patient was willing to pay the difference between the coverage for ambulatory surgery and an overnight stay in the hospital, then the insurance company would drop its coverage of the procedure completely. In other words, it would not pay anything if the patient or family offered to pay out-of-pocket for a hospital stay proposed by the surgeon.

Instead of arguing this issue as patient advocates, administrators resorted to their usual resourcefulness, "managing" this problem instead of solving it. They invented a new class of hospital admission, which they labeled "observation status" (OBS) or "twenty-three-hour admission." They ruled that a hospital stay of less than twenty-four hours would be considered an outpatient or ambulatory basis, and not an inpatient or admission basis. In reality, nobody planned to count the hours of the hospital stay, and many OBS patients ended up staying more than the twenty-three-hour limit allowed. Indeed, this plan was a face-saving farce for the insurance companies. OBS patients would occupy regular hospital beds, but on record they would remain outpatients. This procedure revealed that administrators' priority was to maintain an appearance of propriety. Their main concern was that the hospital, when reviewed, would appear to be compliant, so that the administrators would receive a good grade in their evaluations.

The insurance companies approved the twenty-three-hour observation plan, with the proviso that the decision to resort to this option could only be made a few hours after surgery, *not* before it. In other words, they wouldn't allow doctors to exercise their medical judgment about the length of hospital stays. In essence, the companies decided that doctors' judgments about preventative hospital admissions were now invalid. Instead, they wanted doctors to only make "reactive" decisions—to allow admission only after "finding or discovering" (or inventing) a good medical reason for an OBS hospital stay, which would not be *called* an admission.

This proviso, in turn, caused hospitals and doctors to resort to all manner of expensive games to meet its requirements on paper. For example, it is well known that there is about a 5 percent chance of postoperative bleeding after a tonsillectomy, especially in adults; in many doctors' opinions, that risk warrants an overnight hospital stay for all patients undergoing such surgeries. But the insurers disagreed. Likewise, if a surgeon recommends a stay or a patient decides to stay an extra day in the hospital for valid nonmedical reasons (such as being concerned about living alone, needing to drive several hours to get home, fear of possible complications, or a panic attack), the insurance company will object and refuse coverage. In logistical terms, it seems perfectly obvious that if, for example, a patient lives alone and a hundred miles away from a hospital in a rural area, he should be afforded the preventative care of an overnight stay; if complications arose at home, help could come too late.

Because insurance companies will not acknowledge such concerns, doctors have had to invent or find reasons for admission that the insurance companies will consider valid. To facilitate the invention of such reasons, hospital administrators have circulated lists of "acceptable"—but not necessarily true—reasons to justify a twenty-three-hour hospital or OBS stay. In my specialty, ENT, the list of acceptable indications includes bleeding, nausea, vomiting, dizziness, the need for intravenous medications, and respiratory monitoring of sleep apnea. All of these are often used as bogus reasons that mask an underlying, medically valid reason that would not be accepted by the insurance company.

Sometimes, it is not the hospitals but rather the insurers themselves that coach doctors to "find" such invalid reasons. Indeed, I first learned of the ways to get around the requirements of the twenty-three-hour stay in 1986, shortly after my arrival to Boston. I called to object to an insurance company's refusal to cover hospital admission for an adult patient on whom I planned to perform a tonsillectomy. A sympathetic employee of the company who answered my call informed me that he had to comply with his company's policies and deny my admission request as it was presently worded. But he did not hesitate to teach me how I could get around the policy and admit my patient to the hospital for the tonsillectomy. He instructed me to register the patient for surgery as an ambulatory patient, and then to write an order after surgery to admit him to the hospital for bleeding—even if there was no bleeding. He assured me that nobody would ever check. I was first shocked and then surprised. But I did it anyway. It worked, and I have been repeating this process since, like many of my colleagues. To the best of my knowledge, nobody has ever checked, objected, or complained about this unethical practice.

Such "games," of course, always create difficulties on top of difficulties. In this case, the proviso about finding "valid reasons" for twenty-three-hour stays resulted not only in doctors inventing hard-to-disprove reasons for admissions, but also in new, expensive transfer procedures. In particular, the insurers' clause that a reason for admission must be found after surgery, not before, created a second difficulty for doctors. Many simply lacked the time to unnecessarily check on all their patients, who may not be close enough to the operating rooms, after surgery and then write out an order. So, the administrators obliged through yet another little game: they decided that an order for a twenty-three-hour observation could be written while the patient was still in the operating room (OR), but as a separate, *untimed* order. In other words, hospitals coached doctors to write and sign orders, which would normally be written in the recovery room after surgery, as independent entries before the patient left the OR. This saved the surgeon a trip to the recovery room. But to maintain the appearance of compliance, new logistical procedures had to be created to accommodate this policy. The most efficient practice—allowing these patients to go from the recovery room to a hospital bed—had to be abandoned, because it would make it obvious that the decision to admit them had already been made. So instead, such patients were transferred to a newly created station so that the decision to admit them for observation would appear to have been made after surgery. After that, they were transferred *again* to an inpatient hospital bed on another floor.

Of course, all these extra transfers incurred extra charges. In other words, hospitals "managed" the problem, and found, at the same time, a convenient way to increase their income, and therefore costs. Thus, the twenty-three-hour observation, which was created in response to insurers' efforts to cut costs, ultimately allowed hospital administrators to charge extra for patient transfers and admissions, and gave insurers justification for raising their premiums. For example, after this policy was adopted in the late eighties, patients at my hospital were charged an extra $600 for the forty-five minutes they spent in the newly created, totally unnecessary step-down recovery room after I operated on them and before they were admitted to twenty-three-hour stays.

In addition to all these unnecessary costs and inconveniences, the games administrators and insurers play with each other encourage a culture of cheating among physicians. For my own part, being an old-timer, I have always admitted all my surgical patients for an overnight stay—and as a result, I've found myself having to bend the rules. In that respect, I'm as guilty as any physician of bending the rules rather than fighting them. For example, to avoid repetitions which might arouse suspicion of noncompliance on my part, I've tried to pick a different reason for observation status each time, be it bleeding, dehydration, nausea, vomiting, or respiratory monitoring. Needless to say, the reason I've picked might not be justifiable, appropriate, or necessary. Indeed, my residents have sometimes asked me sarcastically as they put the final touches on postoperative orders, "What's the reason for the transfer to the observations status today?" I've usually answered, "Pick anything you want from the list." And even as a "chronic abuser" of this type of subterfuge, I have never been called in by administrators for questioning or pressure. But a manager once insinuated to my secretary that if I kept admitting all my surgical cases to the hospital, I would risk losing referrals. This obvious and clear threat turned out to be an empty one, because I continued to admit patients, and my practice didn't suffer. I simply could not change forty-year-old routines that had protected the safety of my patients.

Sadly, the nonsense surrounding twenty-three-hour observations represents only the tip of the iceberg; it is symptomatic of many similar medical policies—and of similar "cheating" practices that grow up in response. For example, most insurers will not cover a routine nasal endoscopy, since they consider it to be a procedure independent of the usual evaluation and management that take place during a routine visit. To be compliant with the insurance companies' requirements, a doctor therefore needs to document the indications every time a nasal endoscopy is performed, so that billing for it will be justifiable. As a result, one needs to come up with reasons for the examination, such as to suction the nose, to have a better inside view, to check for the presence of nasal polyps, or to follow up after sinus surgery. This is redundant and an unnecessary waste of time, because I (and almost all rhinologists) believe that a nasal endoscopy should be performed as a matter of routine on all patients with nasal complaints.

To sum up, it would have been cheaper, less time-consuming, and more honest to tell the insurance companies that their decisions about ambulatory procedures (and about many other areas) were unwise and inapplicable, and then work with them for solutions in the patients' best interests. One can easily imagine the long hours that administrators had to work to design the twenty-three-hour observation plan and negotiate it with the insurance companies. The fact that this plan was worked out in major teaching institutions and leading universities across the nation demonstrates that low ethical standards have been allowed to permeate the most respected sites of academic medicine. If all this time-consuming work and maneuvering is not unethical and dishonest, what is?

In conclusion, insurance companies' power and lobbies have allowed them to enjoy privileges and certain immunities. As result, they are neither pressured nor motivated to shape up and reform. With the obvious government bias for corporations, insurance companies have called the shots so far and gotten away with it; they even *lead* reforms in manners that suit them. Their abuses and inadequacies are common, while the profits they seek are often exorbitant and unethical. They trespass on responsibilities that traditionally belonged to the medical profession, in efforts to reduce their own costs and increase their revenues. The arbitrary power they have been allowed to exercise is a grave mistake that needs to be corrected.

Meanwhile, the medical profession has unfortunately not reacted energetically enough to effectively oppose the insurance companies, leaving the field open for finances and greed to determine health standards and requirements. Instead, medical professionals get around insurance policies, resulting in expensive logistics and a culture of cheating and "smartness." This lack of effective responses to such self-serving, unilateral decisions is only one example of the medical profession's and its leaders' failings in health care, one of this book's theses. The upshot of all of this, of course, is that what is best for the patient has become history; across the nation, individuals who suffer remain unattended to.

Chapter Seven
Pharmaceutical Companies

The for-profit pharmaceutical industry has become an integral part of health care, not only because it researches and manufactures important medications, but because it has infiltrated everything from drug regulations to drug delivery and research. Moreover, it now influences practitioners' behaviors and decisions at the ground level through continuing education, marketing campaigns, and outright favors. In these days of medical commercialization, this sort of "support"—which ranges from sandwiches for residents' luncheons to multimillion-dollar grants for medical research and education—raises enormous conflict-of-interest issues that the medical profession urgently needs to address. But by failing to make adequate or serious attempts to ensure ethical conduct between the medical community and pharmaceutical industry, medical leaders and practitioners have shirked their duty and allowed the time-tested traditions of the Hippocratic Oath to fall by the wayside.

To be fair, I should preface this chapter by stating that the pharmaceutical industry's significant contributions to health care in general over the years are not the subject of any doubt. Medications made possible and available thanks to active, ongoing research continue to save lives and reduce suffering. I would never blame drug companies for doing what is in their own self-interest while also respecting laws and regulations; instead, I blame the health care system for having created and tolerated a climate that facilitated the intrusion, dominance, and corrupt dealings of for-profit corporations in health care delivery, research, and education.

Corporate-sponsored Medical Research.

How did the pharmaceutical industry come to be as powerful and pervasive as it is today? Its present influence represents both historical decisions on the part of the government that resulted in looser regulations and "sweetheart deals," and the failure of medical leaders to acknowledge and resist lucrative but risky changes when they are introduced.

The rapid growth of pharmaceutical research at American universities dates back to 1980, when Congress passed the Bayh-Dole Act, which permitted institutions and researchers to benefit financially if their federally sponsored research resulted in the development of commercial products. This act gave universities, small businesses, and nonprofit organizations control over their intellectual property by allowing them to patent discoveries made with federally funded money.

Since the late twentieth century, biomedical research has grown very quickly, but the available funding from the government has not. As a result, teaching and research institutions have felt compelled to look for other sources of funding. Rich and prosperous drug companies have been more than happy to step into the gap and offer financial help. This trend continues to the present day. For example, when the National Institutes of Health (NIH) cut research funding in 2006 for the first time in three decades, following a two-year period of level funding, this proved to be a golden opportunity for the pharmaceutical industry to move even further into research and teaching, increasing its grip on health care.

The influence of the for-profit pharmaceutical industry *cannot* be overstated: it is solely responsible for the development of most of the medications available today in the United States, while research supported by the NIH and other nonindustry sources is responsible for only a small percentage. But these statistics are deceptive; we should not forget that the pharmaceutical industry benefits enormously from publicly funded research, tax breaks, and other business advantages while reaping large profits.

One can easily imagine the risks that medical research is facing in the long term, given this state of affairs. Indeed, in 2000 the editor in chief of the *New England Journal of Medicine* expressed her concern that academic centers, by allowing themselves to become research outposts for industries, contribute to an overemphasis on drugs and devices.[57] To

---

57 Angell, "Academic Medicine," 1516–18.

put that emphasis in terms of dollar figures, let me repeat a statistic: in 1980, drug expenditures by patients were $12 billion; by 2002, the figure climbed to $162 billion, a 1,250 percent increase.[58] In 1980, spending on drugs accounted for 4.9 percent of total health care outlays; by 2004, the figure came close to 15 percent.[59] How do these sorts of burgeoning costs come about? There are many answers, but one might be that the emphasis on researching "lucrative" products has resulted in not-always-necessary increases in drug costs. To see how this works in terms of specifics, let's take the example of a drug for diabetes. In 2006, the FDA approved a new drug, Januvia, to control blood sugar levels with supposedly fewer side effects than older drugs. Manufactured by Merck, the drug costs between three and four dollars per day.[60] Older diabetic drugs can cost as little as fifty cents per day. Is the increase in cost justifiable here? Probably not. This example illustrates how drug companies set the priorities in research and aggressive marketing. The unavoidable results are higher health care costs that do not necessarily improve health care. I can provide a personal example of unfair drug pricing; I take Norvasc daily, a medication for high blood pressure. When I buy a three-month supply, the tablets cost me 16.6 cents each. Once, my order was late arriving, and I needed to buy five tablets to use until it arrived. My local pharmacy charged me $2.25 per tablet. This example illustrates the very wide range of pricing that is hard to understand and justify.

Not only has the direction of research been shifted from prevention and utility toward profitable products, but also unfavorable and neutral research results have sometimes been suppressed, distorted, or falsely advertised, to the detriment of the public health. Indeed, the independence and objectivity of researchers, which used to be ensured and protected by financial support from government organizations, nonprofit organizations, and universities, has become a thing of the past. No wonder, therefore, that pervasive biases have crept into medical research and its outcomes. Doctors who accept money from drug companies in order to invest in their own research laboratories and who design and manufacture medical appliances are especially vulnerable to behaviors that constitute flagrant conflicts of interest. As a result, the issue of how medical research results

---

58 Barlett and Steele, *Critical Condition*, 35.

59 Ibid.

60 Associated Press, "New Oral Diabetes Drug Gets FDA Approval," MSNBC. com, October 17, 2006.

are analyzed, reported, and made available to the public has become a matter of grave concern. Research results that could be unfavorable to a funding company may be withheld or never published, and employees of the companies themselves may even be the ones responsible for collecting the research data and analyzing it.[61]

Results may be distorted to seem favorable in journal articles, in ads aimed at doctors, and in ads aimed at the general public. For example, an article in the *Boston Globe* in 2000 cited a study conducted between 1990 and 1996 which showed that "pharmaceutical companies refused to allow researchers to publish data unfavorable to the company's products."[62] This article also cited two important studies to illustrate the biased influence of the industry. The first study reviewed reports of 196 tests conducted on nonsteroid, anti-inflammatory drugs. It found that 76 percent of the articles about these tests contained doubtful or invalid statements. The second study reviewed 809 articles published in major medical journals, revealing that 29 percent of them had "guest or ghost authors." Guest authors are usually experts who allow their names to be used as authors to enhance the credibility of scientific papers, for a fee. Ghost authors are hired by companies to write articles anonymously.

The suffering and even deaths such misrepresentations and suppressions have caused or contributed to have been the subject of many lawsuits. Wyeth promised to set aside $16 billion by 2003 to dispose of well-publicized lawsuits by patients who developed heart-valve disease after using Phen-Fen,[63] which was marketed as a medication for weight reduction. By 2007, the $16 billion sum went up to $21 billion.[64] It is hard to believe that *none* of the researchers at Wyeth and *none* of the prescribing doctors were aware of this complication before it became widely known many victims later. Indeed, such widespread damage to consumers' health could only have occurred through the suppression of research data.

Going hand in hand with the suppression of unfavorable data at the

61   Susan Okie, "A Stand for Scientific Independence; Medical Journals Aim to Curtail Drug Companies' Influence," *Washington Post*, August 5, 2001.

62   Alice Dembner, "Internist Hits Pharmaceutical Industry," *Boston Globe*, August 16, 2000.

63   Barlett and Steele, *Critical Condition*, 220.

64   Evelyn Pringle, "No End in Sight for Fen-Phen Lawsuits," LawyersandSettlements. com, January 29, 2007, http://www.lawyersandsettlements.com/articles/00575/pph-lawsuits.html.

clinical level is the suppression and distortion of research results when presented to the public in the form of advertising. Sometimes, these ads are manipulative and deceptive, to the detriment of the public's health. Premature ads for new, inadequately tested medications can result in skyrocketing sales; patients see ads for new medications and request them, even before the doctors know much about them, and before enough evidence has been accumulated about their safety, advantages, and possible complications. The story of the Phen-Fen medication mentioned earlier illustrates this point. Some ads even offer free samples (for example, Imitrex has been offered for migraines, Cialis has been offered for erectile dysfunction, and Nexium has been offered for stomach acid reflux). Such offers are tantamount to practicing medicine without a license. The usual "ask your doctor" mantra at the end of such ads ends up being only a pro forma, legal bulletproofing measure. Meanwhile, statements like "My son's life could have been saved had that particular drug been released earlier" are common. Such statements conceal the dark underside of biased research: how many people have died or suffered from unexpected complications of newly released drugs? Indeed, it is often only after considerable suffering that the evidence for serious complications emerges and becomes known. The medicalization of the normal aging processes, without solid scientific evidence, is one illustrative example of this process. The use of hormones in menopausal women had been advertised successfully. But since then, evidence has surfaced that artificial hormones may increase the incidence of breast cancer, heart disease, and pulmonary embolisms. How many women have suffered as a result? We will never know.

The medical advertising industry took off as a result of loosened regulation. In 1997, the FDA opened the doors for medical companies to advertise directly to consumers on TV. This advertising has been abused to such an extent that it has come to represent a public disservice—not to mention a health hazard. The FDA is supposed to monitor the ads for misleading information about medications it has approved, but its budget restrictions for this responsibility mean this monitoring was never intended to be serious. Indeed, in general the FDA is unable to enforce its own regulations; drug companies do not conform to agreements made with the FDA regarding follow-up studies that are supposed to be conducted after drugs are allowed on the market. Two out of three studies have not even begun.[65] The FDA is so overwhelmed with requests and pressures to

---

65   Andrew Bridges, "FDA Says Firms Still Lagging on Follow-Up Drug Studies," *Boston Globe*, March 4, 2006.

approve new drugs that its approval is no longer a guarantee of safety. It is under constant pressure from the pharmaceutical companies to release new drugs faster.

Fraudulent marketing schemes are constantly being hatched, as numerous lawsuits against pharmaceutical companies, even the giant ones, have demonstrated. For example, in 2007 the *Boston Globe* reported that Bristol-Myers and a subsidiary agreed to pay $515 million to settle civil suits over fraudulent drug marketing and pricing schemes, including illegally promoting an antipsychotic drug to children and the elderly, between the years 2000 and 2005. The government did not pursue criminal charges; the sales force was assigned the blame for fraud practiced over a five-year period.[66] As far as I'm aware, none of these illegal activities resulted in criminal charges or managers being fired or going to jail. Instead, regardless of civil penalties and huge fines, the pharmaceutical industry continues to flourish as one of the fastest-growing industries.

Rising Drug Prices

Another way in which the government has failed to curb pharmaceutical companies' self-interest has been in regard to drug pricing. Earlier I mentioned that pharmaceutical companies have been allowed to determine the direction of medical research at universities, and as a result have encouraged the replacement of older, cheaper, and effective medicines with more expensive versions that may not be substantially better. In addition to this influence on research, they also seem to be able to effectively lobby the government when it comes to unfair drug prices. As an example of the sweetheart deals the industry receives, Congress passed legislation preventing Medicare, the biggest national health care provider, from negotiating favorable deals with the pharmaceutical industry. In contrast, private insurers can negotiate deals, and as a result they save significantly. Why not Medicare? Our capitalist system should not be allowed to function against the interests of the government and the people, like it does.

Pharmaceutical companies go beyond influencing regulations and current laws; they may also ignore even those that exist. For example, the government alleged in 2009 that the pharmaceutical company Wyeth cheated the government by avoiding paying hundreds of millions of dollars

---

66 J. Salzman and L. Lowalczyk, "Drug Firm, Subsidiary Settle Suits for $515 m. Prices Scheme, Fraud Alleged," *Boston Globe*, September 29, 2007.

in rebates to Medicaid.[67] The company offered significant discounts to hospitals for medications to suppress stomach acidity, but failed to offer the same discounts to state Medicaid programs as required by law. As another example, the Associated Press reported in 2001that TAP Pharmaceutical Products paid $885 million to settle allegations that it inflated prices and bribed doctors to prescribe its prostate-cancer drug Lupron.[68]

Infiltration of Medicine

The failures on the part of the medical profession, hospitals, administrators, and government bureaucrats to intervene and prevent such improprieties and conflicts of interest represent very serious abdications of leadership. Instead, leaders respond by "managing" problems or going around them instead of preventing and solving them—one theme of this book. In order to look "clean" and to protect themselves, the different parties involved in medical research generate volumes of regulations. But since these regulations are written by the parties themselves (universities, teaching institutes, and so forth), it is extremely doubtful that they can police themselves effectively, especially when they have a financial interest in the research being conducted on their premises and in its outcome. And in the absence of ongoing monitoring by the leaders on-site, regulations remain ineffective—even more so when large institutions themselves are the beneficiaries. Indeed, no matter how strict rules are, it is always possible for beneficiaries to discover and adopt smart and apparently legal ways to circumvent them, and to find loopholes to hide behind when they come under fire. When there are suspicions of improprieties, more or stricter regulations are generated. But there are no compliance officers to monitor violations, as there are for monitoring billing. And even if there were officers, not all violations of rules and ethics by individual doctors and institutions are easily noticeable or preventable. It is interesting to note that the honor system is judged acceptable when it comes to research, but is considered totally unacceptable when it comes to billing.

To give an example of the ineffective regulations and "suggestions" that medical leaders come up with, in August 2000, the NIH convened a national conference on conflicts of interest. Evidence was presented about

---

67 Devlin Barrett, "Drug Firm Wyeth Accused of Defrauding Medicaid," *Boston Globe*, May 19, 2009.

68 Ibid.

the risks of research funded by pharmaceutical companies and conducted by investigators with financial stakes in the outcome. Concern was also expressed about medical articles written by "ghost authors" or published under the name of "guest authors" in exchange for honoraria. One radical proposal put forth during that meeting called for drug companies to turn over final testing of new drugs to the NIH, with the drug companies providing the funding. The drug industry succeeded in killing this proposal, and insisted instead that simple disclosures of conflicts of interest in publications would be enough to handle possible conflicts of interest. It was agreed at this meeting that simple disclosures of conflicts would go a long way toward solving any problems, and that radical, preventive proposals would be impractical. But this is certainly not correct; mandated disclosures of financial connections with pharmaceutical, medical device, or biotechnological industries have not proven to be enough to address the dangerous conflicts of interest that researchers, teachers, and authors face. In 2009, the *Boston Globe* reported that one Massachusetts psychiatrist had been paid by the pharmaceutical industry over $1.5 million in fees between 2000 and 2007. He defended himself in statements and letters, saying that he had been conscientious about disclosure requirements.[69]

Doctors who attend a professional meeting or read a medical journal do not pay attention to the small print where disclosures are usually made, nor do they act like possible prosecutors or critical reviewers every time they read an article. Perhaps they should, but they do not. There is always an assumption that what is printed or presented has passed a rigorous peer review process, but unfortunately, this is not always so. I and other doctors can tell stories of colleagues who are not truthful or candid when they are trying to market a surgical technique or a device they invented before its value has been proven. Chapter 8, which concerns sinusitis, has many illustrations to prove this point. Simply stated, disclosures have failed to work.

To be fair, I should note that, occasionally, efforts to address conflicts of interest in medical research are made, but these prove to be more pro forma than effective, because of the absence of effective monitoring systems and common human failings. In 2007, Partners of Massachusetts put a disclosure form on its web site to be filled out by providers, administrators, and even trustees. The aim was to "identify, review, and manage any relationship that could create a conflict of interest." This measure was a

---

69   Liz Kowalczyk, "Partners Curbs Doctors' Drug Industry Ties," *Boston Globe*, April 10, 2009.

step in the right direction, but its language rendered it suspect: it talked about "managing" a conflict of interest, and not attempting to prevent it. Nor did this measure address the risks involved when Partners itself has a possible conflict of interest—when it becomes the defendant and the jury at the same time. Therefore, as one might expect, the result of these disclosure forms has been limited at best. Likewise, Partners' efforts to curb physicians' drug industry ties have been ineffective. Partners ruled, totally arbitrarily, that one or two company-sponsored presentations by physicians would be allowed per year, but repeated lectures paid for by the same company would not be allowed, and that hospital oversight of these activities would be more rigorous. However, the physicians were still allowed to act as paid consultants;[70] thus, these reforms fail to address the heart of the matter. I doubt that a new, costly layer of bureaucracy will ever be created to ensure compliance with these rules and requirements, which are piled on top of so many other pro forma, bulletproofing measures that collect dust on unused shelves.

Another, earlier attempt was suggested in 2001 to address conflicts of interest. Prominent medical leaders called for the creation of independent research institutes by universities and their industrial partners. These research institutes would be totally new entities that would be entirely separate from universities to ensure better objectivity and the effective prevention of conflicts of interest. But no such institutes have been created to date. One of the authors, the then-faculty dean of Harvard Medical School, failed to take action when he could have.[71] Sadly, it is naïve to expect that the donor industries will fully and conscientiously cooperate with this project, if it is ever implemented.

Some leaders actually try to put a positive spin on this issue. As an example, the Massachusetts General Physicians Organization (MGPO) has run articles in its newsletter stating that collaborations between companies and heath care providers represent positive and beneficial developments; its only caveat is that "everyone needs to know how to navigate these relationships successfully."[72] This caution is more pro forma than serious, applicable, or enforceable. It illustrates how leaders, especially those with a

---

70   Ibid.

71   Hamilton Moses III and Joseph B. Martin, "Academic Relationships with Industry: A New Model for Biomedical Research," *Journal of the American Medical Association* 285, no. 7 (2001): 933–35.

72   Massachusetts General Physicians Organization, "Reality or Perception," MGPO Newsletter, October 2007.

conflict of interest, actually embrace risky relationships with corporations in health care, rather than fighting or reforming them. Likewise, in his 2005 spring message, the president of the American Rhinologic Society wrote to members about his achievements, "which include both scientific and social programs as well as enhanced corporate support [that] will provide a building scaffold for the next fifty years."[73] He was, of course, referring to the growing but unnecessary trend of generous corporate support of professional meetings.

On the other hand, Stanford University School of Medicine and Memorial Sloan-Kettering Cancer Center in New York City saw the need to go further and simply banned industry support of specific continuing medical education (CME) courses for doctors and courses altogether.[74]

So far, I've discussed how pharmaceutical companies influence the practice of medicine through directly paying doctors as consultants or researchers or speakers, and through marketing campaigns in the form of direct advertisements and CME courses. But pharmaceutical companies go beyond this; they also actively court doctors through what amounts to indirect pay—through freebies, gifts, perks, paid vacations, and other luxuries. It all amounts to subtle—and not so subtle—bribery. Perks vary from little details—sandwich luncheons for residents, umbrellas, electronic devices at conferences, tickets to sports events—to generous fees for consulting, speaking honoraria, and travel to plush resorts with all expenses paid. And when it comes to the big league, perks take the form of major, "unrestricted" grants, fellowships, funds for medical equipment, and so forth. Aside from the costs to the patient in terms of quality of care, let us not forget that such bribes, by being so widespread and expensive, contribute to the rising costs of health care. Indeed, the large sums spent on perks amount to a major blow to the respectability of the medical profession.

Why do pharmaceutical companies get away with such blatant practices which may be considered bribery? Until recently, there seemed to be no restrictions on the perks doctors can receive from pharmaceutical companies. However, some hospitals have now banned these companies from sponsoring resident lunches or dinners. Indeed, to revisit the theme of the impossibilities of the current self-regulation, let's take the example of

---

73   http://www.american-rhinologic.org/news.0405.presidentsmessage.phtml

74   Liz Kowalczyk, "Partners Curbs Doctors' Drug Industry Ties." *Boston Globe*, April 10, 2009.

the American Medical Association, which mounted a campaign to educate physicians about the ethical guidelines involved in accepting gifts from drug companies. Formulating ethical guidelines might seem like a noble cause—but not so when most of the million-dollar cost for that campaign was paid for by drug companies![75]

Bribes constitute an effective, widespread marketing technique; after all, philanthropy is not the top priority of the drug industry. Indeed, bribes are intended to capture the attention, goodwill, and the ears of doctors—and they succeed. Studies have shown that physicians who accept gifts from drug representatives are more likely to prescribe expensive new drugs, even when the new drugs have little advantage over the cheaper, generic ones.[76] Although there are no obvious strings attached to corporate "gifts," when the time comes to write a prescription, the first medication that comes to a doctor's mind is the one manufactured by the company providing the perks.

As an example of how such perks/bribes work, let's take a typical example: many doctors are offered fully paid weekend trips to exclusive resorts, where they present or listen to lectures about newly developed drugs. These lectures are often little more than advertisements, often masked by accompanying high-quality presentations by national experts on related subjects. The reason that they're so well-attended is that they're held in resort locations. After all, would a doctor prefer to attend lectures in a hospital auditorium at a low cost to all involved, or to go to the same lectures in Bermuda, Palm Beach, or Las Vegas, with all expenses paid? Even when lectures are held on-site, they tend to be lavish. For example, the Massachusetts General Hospital Allergy and Immunology Department organizes monthly, city-wide Allergy-Immunology rounds in Boston. These rounds are held in a plush hotel and include drinks, buffet dinners, and free parking. These rounds are supported by an unrestricted educational grant from the pharmaceutical giant GlaxoSmithKline.

I would not want to give the impression in this chapter that I myself have been immune to the marketing techniques of pharmaceutical companies. So, as a more personal example, I'd like to describe the ways in which I have been influenced. I was first introduced to the world of pharmaceutical favors when I accepted an invitation, in the late eighties,

---

75   Susan Okie, "AMA Criticized for Letting Drug Firms Pay for Ethics Campaign," *Washington Post*, August 30, 2001.

76   Alice Dembner, "Drug Firms Woo Doctors with Perks," *Boston Globe*, May 20, 2001.

to travel to Florida and attend a meeting on the antibiotic treatment of sinusitis, with all expenses paid. The host was the maker of Augmentin, an antibiotic I often prescribed for sinus infections, and the conference was high quality and luxurious, to say the least. For a few years thereafter, like many of my colleagues, I accepted fees from pharmaceutical companies to hold talks and lectures on the subject of my interest, sinusitis, with no strings whatsoever attached. At that point in my life, I hadn't really considered the full ramifications of accepting companies' invitations; after all, I was never directly pressured to "sell" the companies' drugs.

But questions kept recurring in my mind. Is sponsorship of CME by for-profit corporations risk-free? Medical doctors, like other mortals, are vulnerable to temptation and biases. Corporations are not notably benevolent, and their expenditures must be fully justifiable to their investors. An idealistic commitment to continuing medical education is not usually high on their agendas. My doubts became so grave that I found I couldn't even attend medical society meetings or rounds sponsored by corporations without feeling terribly conflicted. In 2004, I attended the fiftieth anniversary meeting of the American Rhinologic Society, of which I was a member before I retired. The meeting, held in New York City, was to commemorate a half century of medical achievements in the field of rhinology. It was very well attended and included representatives from countries all over the world. The presentations and posters provided a comprehensive picture of present-day rhinology and of the latest advances in the diagnosis and management of nasal and sinus patients. The meeting itself was luxurious. The cost of registration for this meeting was minimal, little more than a formality, and what I received in return was very generous indeed. I was given two tickets for a gala dinner sponsored by Merck, and I was also invited to two free breakfast symposia moderated by national experts in the field and sponsored by Abbott Pharmaceuticals and (once again) Merck. Additionally, GE Navigation and Karl Storz Endoscopy cosponsored a gala reception for the attendees. The exhibitors offered boxed lunches during the meeting. Free coffee and soft drinks were available during intermissions.

Although the educational value of the meeting was excellent, I found it extremely disturbing to think that, all too often, there are no unbiased teaching alternatives to meetings like these. Doctors have no choice but to learn about advances and new medicines, their uses, and possible complications from the sellers of the drugs themselves. Furthermore, I reflected that the costs of this meeting had been unjustifiable; after all, were gala dinners and receptions really necessary to get important medical information shared among the medical community?

Because feelings of discomfort and doubt kept nagging me, after a few years, I stopped making myself available for teaching activities sponsored by pharmaceutical companies. Years later, I still wonder whether or not my remunerated participation in such teaching activities meant I sold my soul. I do not think I did. But I admit that, when I had a choice between two antibiotics for sinusitis or between two steroid sprays for nasal allergies, I automatically picked the ones manufactured by my host companies. I continued to do so as a matter of habit, many years after I stopped being a beneficiary of their generosity. I do not think I was being unethical, but those were activities I am still not proud of. And what's even more disturbing to me is the fact that the sort of teaching and lectures I engaged in are considered perfectly normal and accepted by the medical community, and are widespread among so many doctors. To my mind, that is an indication of how far the practice of medicine in its present form has strayed from its ethical traditions.

In conclusion, pharmaceutical companies have assumed a powerful role in health care today, impacting the safety and cost of drugs and raising conflicts of interest in almost every aspect of health care. The present climate of medical commercialization, hospital corporatization, and medical entrepreneurship mean that conflicts of interest have been allowed to become major issues. Meanwhile the imperfection of human nature and the growing dominance of materialism aggravate the risks. Doctors with strict, traditional principles and integrity are less likely to become the victims of such conflicts, but certainly should not be considered immune to it, as the temptations are numerous and readily available. As the reimbursements for medical services drop and the costs of practicing increase, doctors become more vulnerable. The safeguards and regulations that have been put in place are not enough to seriously address conflicts of interest; it is fanciful and naïve to think that regulations alone can effectively prevent or eradicate conflicts of interest. The medical community needs to take it upon itself to address these issues, through the new, capable, committed, and accountable medical leaders this book is advocating. The conflicts of interest that exist in the current relationship between academic researchers need to be eliminated. Disclosures are not enough. Quality, affordable, ethical medicine is at great risk if for-profit pharmaceutical companies are allowed to continue their intimate infiltration of the health care system.

Chapter Eight
The Story of Chronic Sinusitis and Functional Endoscopic Surgery

The sad story of chronic sinusitis and functional endoscopic sinus surgery is worth describing in some detail. When fully told, it illustrates many of the problems that have plagued health care and that this book discusses. As an ENT surgeon, I have witnessed its unhindered growth and development for years; a new theory about the cause of sinusitis and a new surgical technique to cure it were widely adopted fast, without convincing proofs of their value. Evidence against them was suppressed when it surfaced. The medical and hospital leaderships failed to intervene when they should have to monitor quality of care and to control cost. The see-no-evil attitude of medical doctors helped the wide spread of a questionable theory and a questionable surgical technique. The absence of user-friendly venues provided no opportunity for caring and dissenting doctors to speak out against a lucrative doubtful practice. The power of marketing and promotion contributed significantly to the problem. The current malpractice system, which scares doctors, continues to fail as a quality controller in health care.

The saga of chronic sinusitis and FES began during the last three decades of the twentieth century. In the 1970s, Dr. Messerklinger, a noted ENT surgeon from Graz, Austria, repopularized an old idea that infections of the paranasal sinuses were due to anatomic obstructions of a key area inside the nose. This area became known as the ostiomeatal complex (OMC). The idea was that if the OMC was too narrow or closed, sinus secretions and contents would be blocked before they could follow their normal course of draining to the back of the nose (the nasopharynx) and then being swallowed. This blockage, it was postulated, caused irritation, swelling, subsequent infections, and other signs and symptoms of chronic sinusitis. At around the same time, the development of surgical telescopes, or endoscopes, made it feasible for surgeons to more safely and easily act on Messerklinger's theory by surgically widening the OMC. Thus, functional endoscopic sinus surgery (FES) was introduced, and quickly became very popular.

FES and the theory behind it seemed to make a lot of sense, and were therefore widely accepted and adopted in Europe in the eighties, in spite of the fact that neither the theory nor the surgery were actually tested or proven to be consistently effective. Shortly after their acceptance in Europe, Messerklinger's ideas were also popularized in the U.S., as endoscopes (already in use in Europe) finally became widely available here also.

I should state from the beginning that endoscopic sinus surgery in general, but not the so-called functional one, has certainly helped large numbers of suffering patients, and is considered a major advance in the field of rhinology. Endoscopes allow better and safer surgical access to the nasal cavities and easier surgical removal of obstructing and other pathologies in the nose that cause or facilitate persistent sinus infections. They have also been successfully used in removing intranasal tumors and in cranial-base surgeries, with less morbidity than older techniques that require skin cuts and/or craniotomies. The criticisms in this chapter are aimed only at the common *abuses* of functional endoscopic sinus surgery. FES quickly acquired enormous—and in retrospect, suspect—popularity in the U.S. Shortly after its introduction, the reported incidence of sinusitis increased rapidly and for no apparent reason. For example, from 1986 to 1988, the federal government reported fifty million workdays lost to sinusitis. Between 1989 and 1992, the numbers increased to seventy-three million. I suspect that the numbers would not have increased so dramatically had FES not been introduced, aggressively marketed, and popularized. Indeed, because FES was lucrative, its indications were stretched to a suspect extent. Any facial pressures or pains were wrongly ascribed by certain physicians to sinusitis and were considered surgical indications, even in the absence of expected abnormalities on nasal exams and sinus CT scans. Patients frustrated with their treatment-resistant, chronic facial pains were easily convinced to undergo this new, "miraculous" surgical technique.

FES gained popularity among American surgeons through dozens of two- to three-day teaching courses that were offered each year nationwide. The cost of such courses was around $1,500, and the organizers made money for the institutions hosting the courses. Endoscopes manufacturers lent all the instruments needed during the courses to participants for free. The sales of these costly instruments rapidly soared, as one would expect.

FES was publicized through a large number of complimentary presentations in well-attended, national professional meetings. These meetings unfortunately lacked critical reviews and they greatly exaggerated claims about FES. They facilitated the premature marketing of a lucrative surgical technique before it was adequately tested and proven. Likewise, numerous complimentary articles were published prematurely in medical journals, contributing significantly to the sharp rise in the number of sinus surgeries nationwide.

The enthusiasm for FES was such that Medicare and private insurance companies accepted billings for the procedure, even though there was no convincing evidence regarding its efficacy in all patients who were operated upon. Equally surprisingly, this technique did not undergo the scrutiny that is normally required for FDA approval of new medications. Politics and arm-twisting must have played a role in these allowances. The later consequences of FES abuse were, unsurprisingly, never addressed by insurance companies; as the costs of FES escalated, the insurance companies simply responded by raising their rates, rather than trying to control costs by prescreening patients and working on a list of valid indications prepared by responsible professionals from all around the nation.

In 1986, I, like hundreds of my colleagues, did not foresee the abuses that would follow in the wake of FES's increasing popularity. We became interested in this new surgery because it seemed logical and promised to cure the frustrating problems of chronic sinusitis by directly addressing its supposed main cause: an obstruction in key areas of the nose. In the late eighties, I took courses in FES, read a great deal of the literature on the subject, and dissected specimens independently. I also spent several days at the Johns Hopkins Hospital to observe Dr. David Kennedy operating, and later following up with his patients in the outpatient clinic. (Dr. Kennedy is rightfully credited with introducing and popularizing FES in the U.S.)

It took me several months to become comfortable with this new technique, after which period I started using it in the operating room. At first, I used it very conservatively, because I knew it could potentially have serious complications. Operating in such close proximity to the eyes and the brain made blindness, intracranial complications, and even death very real possibilities (the risks increased, of course, in unskilled hands). A couple of years later, when I felt I'd acquired sufficient mastery of the technique, several of my colleagues and I, out of conviction, started organizing teaching courses ourselves in Boston. These were always very well attended.

In the nineties, however, many surgeons, including myself, gradually developed opinions about FES that were different from the dominant ones, which were all overwhelmingly positive. First, we noticed that, although we used the technique carefully and became quite practiced in it, our success rates did not compare well with reported and published ones. For my own part, after I'd enthusiastically performed surgeries for a couple of years, I observed that FES was not always delivering the expected and reported cures. The follow-up data on my cases were not as good as those reported in meetings and the literature. When I compared notes with colleagues, I found out that many shared my skepticism. I became alarmed by the large numbers of sinus surgeries performed nationwide with doubtful or suspect indications, and by the absence of convincing, serious, long-term studies to confirm the value of these surgeries.

We also started observing that certain overconfident surgeons who had not adequately educated or trained themselves were performing this surgery. In effect, they were simply capitalizing on FES's popularity. As a result, the incidence of serious complications rose quickly. In the nineties, FES was the number one reason that ENT surgeons were taken to court for alleged malpractice.

Unfortunately, my critical colleagues and I were denied adequate forums to publically express our dissenting opinions and observations. I wrote critical papers that were constantly turned down by medical journals. Indeed, the literature continued to be very positive and to ignore the dissenting opinions of many respected doctors. I began to suspect that some editors were following an unwritten policy of promoting sinus surgeries; I found no other plausible explanation for the remarkable absence of papers critical of FES, its overuses, and its abuses. (In retrospect, my personal previous experiences with other new surgical techniques, which were promoted as miracles but which never stood the test of time and were quickly forgotten, probably helped me to recognize the signals that something was fishy when it came to FES. For example, I had witnessed surgical techniques performed in large numbers to treat vertigo, with original "excellent" results reported, eventually fall into disrepute.)

This suppression of critical opinions eventually led many doctors to give up fighting against the abuses of FES. The medical and business beneficiaries of this "miraculous" surgery are too mighty to fight; they have a whole arsenal of political, legal, and monetary weapons with which to resist control and regulation. A system that does not provide a forum for critics to be heard or their opinions acted upon is not a good system to protect patients and control cost; it is a system crying out for reform.

Present Treatments of Chronic Sinusitis

Unfortunately, most of the currently published research has had little impact so far in clarifying the definition and treatment of chronic sinusitis and in halting abusive surgery. To this day, different specialties, as well as doctors within the same specialty, continue to disagree on criteria used to diagnose chronic sinusitis. Many doctors continue to lump different diseases and conditions under the heading of sinusitis, including nasal allergies, nasal septal deviations, large turbinates, migraine headaches, and ill-defined, atypical facial pains. This is a source of confusion to doctors and to the public in general, and results in high treatment costs and the continued suffering and frustration of many misdiagnosed, mismanaged patients.

As an example, let's consider a hypothetical patient referred to the prestigious Massachusetts General Hospital (MGH) or to the Massachusetts Eye and Ear Infirmary (MEEI) of Boston, with chronic and refractory facial pressures or pains. This patient will receive different treatments depending on which specialist he is channeled to or happens to see. Many of these specialists will make their decisions based on inadequate knowledge of sinusitis. For example, most allergist-immunologists and infectious disease specialists continue to manage sinusitis cases without learning how to conduct the absolutely necessary intranasal examination before starting treatment. So, if the referral goes to an allergist-immunologist, the patient will receive allergy testing, antiallergic medications, or endless immunotherapy (allergy shots). In contrast, an infectious disease specialist will probably prescribe one or more antibiotics; if oral antibiotics do not seem to work, costly intravenous antibiotics may be administered for as long as six weeks.

If the patient undergoes a CT scan of the sinuses, radiologists have a tendency to report common, normal intranasal variants as pathologies, worthy therefore of surgical intervention. For example, if this hypothetical patient has a nonsignificant retention cyst in one cheek or maxillary sinus, he will probably receive an unnecessary referral to a surgeon and undergo an operation to excise this usually asymptomatic cyst. This is a common occurrence, and one that flies in the face of research that has long since proved that these normal variants do *not* cause sinusitis. Sadly, in addition to those radiologists who are simply unaware of relevant research and common knowledge, a minority of ENT and sinus surgeons contributes to the abuse of sinus surgery, and knowingly recommends and performs surgery even on patients with normal CT scans. To add insult to injury, pathologists continue to report chronic inflammation in normal surgical specimens, as if to provide legal and ethical cover for surgeons who operate on patients with normal sinuses or doubtful sinusitis.

But the story doesn't end there. If our hypothetical patient is referred to a surgeon for an "abnormal" CT scan, he will receive different surgeries depending on the surgeon's expertise. If the surgeon is an otolaryngologist, some kind of sinus surgery may be recommended. If the surgeon is an oral surgeon, he may suspect a TMJ disorder and recommend night guards or even a realignment of the teeth. If the referral is to a pain specialist, the patient may end up receiving physical therapy or even Botox injections!

I have not observed a serious attempt by hospitals to remedy these sorts of confusing and wasteful situations. Instead, I have witnessed the widespread frustration of both doctors and patients. Colleagues have called me before referring some of their difficult cases and informed me that they have already operated two or three times on patients without success and do not know what else to do. My answer has remained the same: a diagnosis is necessary first, before planning management. My experience has proven that many of these patients prove to be sufferers of atypical facial pains, and not of chronic sinusitis; hence, it is no surprise that surgery failed to alleviate their suffering. Atypical facial pains may be due to a variety of causes, singly or combined. The medical profession should invest more time in researching the causes rather than marketing costly new treatments, some of which do not make sense. I have known many such patients who have received all kinds of treatments and undergone all kinds of surgeries, only to emerge with their pains intact or even worse. Furthermore, the rebound pains after abuse of over-the-counter painkillers and addiction to prescribed analgesics need to be kept in mind as possible causes or contributing factors in these frustrated and frustrating sufferers.

The Business of FES

So far, I've outlined how current published research has failed to define chronic sinusitis and to clarify the acceptable indications and timing of sinus surgery. Now, let's look into *why* such a situation has been allowed to happen and persist. The unavoidable conclusion is that the business of medicine has been allowed to dominate.

The business of chronic sinusitis and FES in particular, and the business of medicine in general, would not have been possible were it not for the fact that medical leaders have allowed them to proliferate and turned a blind eye to their many failures and other negative consequences. As a result of the free rein, they have provided hospitals, doctors, and related businesses with opportunities for abuses and malpractices. First, training and credentialing of practicing doctors whose medical school education antedated FES has been woefully neglected,[77] and regulations have been pro forma. Second, misleading, confusing, and even false advertising has proliferated. Third, satellite businesses have flourished. Fourth, a minority of doctors continues to abuse their patients and get away with it.

Since the possible complications of sinus surgeries can be serious, especially when conducted by unskilled surgeons, the failure of medical leaders to ensure even that most basic tenet of medicine—to do no harm—represents a very serious charge. Why have they allowed it, then? Simply put, because sinus operations can bring in several thousands of dollars. All the parties involved seek and welcome that extra income.

Indeed, the only gestures medical leaders have made toward ensuring safe sinus surgeries have been pro forma. When FES first became popular, credentialing bodies in hospitals established prerequisites: surgeons had to prove that they attended a two- or three-day course. But naturally, attending one or even several courses was certainly not enough to qualify a surgeon to perform FES. A few hospitals recognized how inadequate this credentialing process was and added another condition: a novice surgeon had to be monitored by an "expert" for the first few surgeries he performed. This decision turned out to be pro forma as well; it looked good on paper, but was not regularly applied and enforced. Besides, early on, there were no real experts; it was almost like the blind leading the blind.

After this shaky start in training and credentialing, innovative doctors started promoting their own modifications of FES, sometimes before they had been tested or proven beneficial. The business of medicine made this activity possible and acceptable. Meanwhile, fellowships in sinus surgery were created to accommodate young graduates interested in learning more about sinus surgeries and in riding this lucrative wave. Of course, many such fellowships (and their research activities) were very generously

---

77 To clarify, current residents have ample opportunities to learn the technique during their training.

supported by industries involved in sinus surgery. Medical leaders did not intervene, even though conflicts of interest continue to contaminate the teaching, research, and practice of medicine in such fellowships.

Second, misleading promotions of FES—and by that, I include not only advertisements, but also inflated research—have been given free rein. Within a year or two of the introduction of FES, books had already been published promoting it (such timing would be very premature for any kind of new treatment). They included information which proved later to be wrong, but that continues to be referenced and was never corrected.

Not only individual authors and researchers, but also whole medical societies jumped on the advertising bandwagon, acting like salesmen for this "miraculous" and lucrative new surgery. For example, the American Academy of Otolaryngology–Head and Neck Surgery (AAO-HNS) promoted a "Sinus Awareness Month." As recently as 2001, the president of the Academy stated, in his message to the membership, that "This [awareness month] is an extremely important educational activity put forth by the Academy…it highlights a disease that we as a specialty are intimately involved with and for which we provide definitive care."[78] This is deceptive on several levels. First, ENT specialists cannot provide "definitive care" for all cases of sinusitis; care of this complicated and often-mislabeled condition must be multidisciplinary. Second, it implies that "sinus pain" is always due to sinusitis, when in fact, it can be due to many other causes, like migraine variants, stress, neuralgias, and others.

Another example of false advertising by this respected medical society showed up in the cover of the monthly Academy bulletin. This cover featured a diagram of a frowning woman who had placed her four fingers on the middle of her forehead, suggesting a severe headache. One of her cheek sinuses, the maxillary, was depicted half-filled with fluid. The obvious message from the AAO-HNS, the teaching arm of the profession, was that the maxillary sinusitis was the cause of the headache, and that a diagnosis of sinusitis was therefore appropriate—a patently wrong claim.

Third, satellite businesses have flourished around sinus surgery, and since they have not been policed, they have substantially added to the cost of health care through unnecessary or even harmful "services." These businesses provide medical instruments, imaging services, antibiotics, and a host of nasal sprays and solutions. Some make incredibly inflated claims or were even very wrong. For example, a company claimed its sinus aerosol medications were "the most efficient route of administration to

---

78 AAO-HNS, *Bulletin*, February 2001.

treat sinusitis and rhinosinusitis." Sometimes, these inflated ads even take place in respectable medical settings. At a booth at the annual AAO-HNS meeting of 2001, a company, Lumenis, advertised the use of lasers for "quick relief of chronic sinusitis with office-based turbinate reduction and septal spur removal (topical anesthesia)." This advertisement misleadingly used the term "chronic sinusitis"; the technique should have been advertised for the treatment of nasal blockage due to large nasal turbinates or septal deviations, and not for blockage due to sinusitis.

Fourth, as a result of the failure of medical leaders to police sinus surgery, a minority of individual physicians have blatantly abused it. To qualify this statement, I should make it clear that most medical doctors are conscientious and mean well. But a minority of FES abusers—among them prominent surgeons who practice and teach in leading medical schools and teaching hospitals—have largely contributed to the nationwide wave of sinus surgery abuse, surgical complications, and significant rises in health care costs. These surgeons may not be numerous, but their practices are well known and disapproved of within professional circles that have chosen to remain silent and not to get involved.

I have seen a few patients who supposedly underwent one or more surgeries, but who proved later to have untouched sinuses when inspected with endoscopy, studied with CT imaging, and observed at surgery. Some dishonest surgeons have claimed that they operated on the four pairs of sinuses and billed heftily, when they actually hadn't opened any sinus. There is no easy way to prove their cheating, and no leaders bother to try.

Second, some powerful surgeons operate without adequate justification. For example, a chief ENT surgeon in a Massachusetts hospital with a great public reputation as a sinus surgeon was infamous among colleagues for operating on patients with normal sinuses. He intimidated and silenced residents who dared to ask him embarrassing questions about his surgical indications. This surgeon even developed his own highly questionable fifteen-minute technique, which he marketed to the lay press. At a meeting of ENT surgeons in Boston, he had the arrogance to show videos of his surgeries on ten patients who had no recognizable pathologies. When challenged by an attendant at the end of the talk, he did not have a good explanation for why he had operated on the presented cases, but he did not seem embarrassed at all. What he did *not* mention during that meeting was that, although his modification takes ten to fifteen minutes to perform, it is billed as a regular FES, which is normally much more involved and takes much more time. Operating quickly on healthy patients and then billing for a full surgery is an obvious act of cheating, one that would qualify as a criminal act should it ever come under the scrutiny of regulators and law officers.

To date, the small numbers of doctors who perform abusive sinus surgery are still powerful enough professionally to block dissenting voices from being heard and published, even as the evidence against the OMC and its role in sinusitis has mounted. As a result, most doctors, residents, students, and nurses who have witnessed the abuses in the operating rooms have not blown the whistle, or have been ignored when they did. This is a sad corollary of the business of medicine, of a persistent, outdated Hippocratic tradition that requires doctors to defend and protect each other, and of the increasing influence of administrators' focus on the bottom line.

Equally destructive has been the influence of these powerful doctors on their trainees. A skilled surgeon I know once advised a fellowship trainee to avoid operating on patients with *normal* sinus CT scans "early in her career," implying that she could get away with it later on, when she had established a reputation. He added that he could get away with it himself, because he was known as the best sinus surgeon in town. Quite a role model for a training fellow in a prestigious hospital!

As another example of unethical "training," I once heard from residents about a young doctor who had just finished his ENT training in Boston. He wanted to specialize in sinus surgery; at that point, he didn't realize what he was in for. Then, he went to Chicago for a one-year sinus surgery fellowship with a famous surgeon in a reputed teaching hospital. After spending a few months with that famous surgeon, he decided to quit because he could neither understand nor tolerate the large numbers of unnecessary surgeries that he was witnessing and performing. Out of a sense of responsibility, he even went to the dean of the medical school there to complain. To my knowledge, the only response administrators made was to grant the young doctor permission to resign without prejudice.

So far, I've outlined the ways in which FES has proven to be big business while failing to consistently provide help, and how both individuals and organizations abuse it. But FES can have far more serious consequences: it can actively harm patients' health. Huge numbers of patients have undergone unnecessary, incomplete, or unsuccessful surgeries and have developed serious and lifelong complications. Tragically, their plight continues to be ignored. The only awareness the public has of this problem is of the minority of cases that are publicized in the media. A very small percentage of patients are angry enough to go through the long, expensive, intimidating, and painful (though possibly lucrative) process of suing. Besides, our legal system does not guarantee that even clearly justified lawsuits will prevail in court.

Individual Activism

When I became aware of the many problems and issues surrounding FES, I tried personally to address them, within my capabilities. My efforts included founding two centers at the hospital where I worked, the Sinus Center and the Atypical Facial Pain Clinic, to conduct studies and to teach.

The Sinus Center brought together a group of different specialists involved in the diagnosis and management of chronic sinusitis. In addition to ENT surgeons, the center had an allergist-immunologist, an infectious disease specialist, a neuro-radiologist, and a pathologist. MEEI, with all its resources, was an ideal venue for this center.

Our goals were to discuss and debate difficult cases, to better define the currently loose diagnosis of chronic sinusitis, and to determine acceptable indications for sinus surgery. Eventually, we hoped to formulate a long-term follow-up protocol, to confirm or raise doubts once and for all about the questionable "excellent" results of FES that were regularly reported in meetings and published in medical journals.

That Sinus Center got off to a great start; all the participants were enthusiastic. The patients referred to the center were mostly suffering women, who'd been diagnosed and previously treated as if they had "chronic sinusitis." In most cases, their conditions had not improved after one or more surgeries, and some had actually gotten worse postoperatively.

It did not take long to reach the conclusion that most of these patients were sufferers of chronic facial pressures and headaches, and that these pains were not related to chronic sinusitis. We based this conclusion on our discovery that these patients had had normal endoscopic intranasal examinations and normal sinus CT scans or MRIs; these findings made the diagnosis of sinusitis very unlikely. Chronic facial pressures and headaches are not necessarily always related to chronic sinusitis, and we were able to understand why years of treatment with medications and sinus surgeries had not helped.

Unfortunately, the center lasted only for a couple of years. Although we made important observations together, the enthusiasm of certain participants in the Sinus Center soon waned when they realized the implications of our observations meant they would have to change their own understanding and management of sinusitis. Moreover, they judged the carefully designed follow-up protocols, meant to provide long-term data on all or a significant number of our patients, to be impractical. I made every effort to sustain the center, but the leaders at MEEI did not see the need to intervene at my request to help keep the center functioning to advance knowledge, improve the quality of care, and help cut costs. The excuse I was given was that it was not the center's responsibility to influence the behavior of doctors or to police them. I thought otherwise, but could do no more. I subsequently dissolved it. It was, however, kept on paper, for marketing purposes. I continued to get referrals as the director of a center that no longer existed.

My second attempt to help frustrated patients who continued to suffer from pain after undergoing FES was to establish the Atypical Facial Pain Clinic, staffed by representatives of the following disciplines: ENT, neurology, dentistry, oral surgery, pain medicine, behavioral psychology, and physical therapy. Patients referred to us were evaluated by all the participants together over forty-five minute periods, and an appropriate management strategy was developed by all participants.

Through observation in this clinic, we affirmed that many conditions that may mimic sinusitis present with facial pressures or pains, nasal congestion, and even postnasal drip. These conditions include migraines and their many variants, TMJ (temporo-mandibular-joints) disorders, myofascial pains, allergies, depression, rebound pains after prolonged use of analgesics, and addictions. These observations reinforced my conviction that a multidisciplinary approach is needed to handle these frustrated and frustrating patients; each of these conditions requires a totally different management strategy. And even with all the multidisciplinary expertise available, we have to admit that we *still* do not have the answer for all these conditions; I have seen patients who failed to respond to all that Western medicine has to offer respond favorably to acupuncture or to other alternative types of medicine.

This clinic helped to reinforce the bottom line: appropriate consultations and proper diagnoses have to be made before management is planned and sinus surgery performed.

I also sought to better understand chronic sinusitis through research. I once performed a study of about one hundred patients who had undergone

FES at MEEI over two successive months. I reviewed their pre-op sinus CT scans and found out that around half of them had normal sinuses or minor, nonsignificant abnormalities. These findings suggested strongly that there were no definite indications for 50 percent of the surgeries performed.

I considered it a duty to publicize my findings about chronic sinusitis, in order to change widely held, erroneous perceptions. But in trying to do so, I ran up against active suppression, roadblocks, and disinterest—just as have other researchers who reached similar conclusions and who've tried to make their findings known. I reported this study at one of MEEI's well-attended weekly teaching activities, the Clinico-Pathologic Conference (CPC). Since I considered it scandalous that surgeons at a well-respected hospital were conducting operations to widen nasal passages that were, in fact, unobstructed and normal, I believed and hoped that my findings would stimulate significant discussions and reactions. I was surprised to discover that I was wrong. The discussion I was hoping to stimulate by shocking the audience never occurred. Colleagues who I knew shared my opinion did not speak out. The only response I got was that "the jury is still out on this issue." Full stop. I did not think so. This lack of reaction, to my mind, compellingly illustrates the fact that the business of medicine currently takes precedence over the science of medicine, even in reputed teaching institutions. What a shame.

As a counterpoint to this lack of reaction to my research on the domestic front, my findings have been very well received by a much larger national and international audience. I was once invited to participate in an international rhinology meeting in Washington DC. I was given the privilege of picking the subject I wanted. I chose to speak about FES, and titled my presentation, "The Facts and Fancy of Functional Endoscopic Sinus Surgery." I openly criticized the epidemic of unnecessary sinus surgeries performed nationally in the United States. I had never experienced as much applause in my academic life after any presentation, and many doctors I did not know stood in line to congratulate me on my "courage" in speaking openly against the widespread abuse of sinus surgeries. It is interesting to note that, in comparison to this response, the much less strongly worded papers that I had submitted for publication in the U.S. were turned down with little explanation. I can only conclude that I was swimming against the prevalent current, and that it is politically incorrect to publish criticisms of FES.

The Continuing Saga

Sadly, FES abuse has not only continued to the present day, it has also spawned other suspect surgical techniques that capitalize on FES's popularity. For example, in 2006, the *American Journal of Rhinology*, the official publication of the American Rhinological Society, published a very premature report about the safety and feasibility of a new surgical technique for endoscopic sinus surgery, called balloon sinuplasty.[79] The technique lacked any valid theoretical base. It claimed to cure sinusitis-like symptoms by widening "abnormally narrow sinus ostia," when no previous research has ever shown narrow ostia to be the cause of any problems. The study was funded by the manufacturer of the balloons needed for the technique, Acclarent, and its authors both accepted consulting fees from this company; one even had an equity position in the company, which he called "small." To add credibility to the report, the manufacturer stated that this technology was "FDA-cleared," whatever that meant. The Federal Drug Administration (FDA) is the federal government agency that has to approve medications and their indications before they are allowed to be sold. Its responsibilities do not include clearing or approving surgical techniques.

Shortly after the balloon sinuplasty was marketed, the *New York Times* ran an article decrying this new technique, stating, "Balloon sinuplasty [is] an example of how the loose regulation of medical devices can enable procedures to be adopted more on the basis of astute marketing than clinical science."[80] Little wonder Acclarent has been so aggressive in trying to convince both patients and doctors of the validity of its technique; the company stands to make a lot of money. Acclarent requires sinus specialists who want to receive training in this technique to make an up-front purchase of $20,000 worth of Acclarent's equipment, including the catheters and balloons needed. Each system is thrown out after a single use, and costs around $1,200. Thankfully, Acclarent has not proven to be very successful in its marketing campaign. With more aggressive marketing, it may in the future, if the current health care landscape persists.

To sum up, FES today continues to be abused, scandalous, risky,

---

79 William E. Bolger and Winston C. Vaughan, "Catheter Based Dilation of the Sinus Ostia: Initial Safety and Feasibility Analysis in a Cadaver Model," *American Journal of Rhinology* 20, no. 3 (2006): 290.

80 Reed Abelson, "Too Soon to Breathe Easy?" *New York Times*, May 4, 2006.

and costly. The new medical leaders this book proposes should be able to act responsibly and put endoscopic sinus surgery back on its appropriate track. The current absence of responsible and concerned medical leaders, a leitmotif of this book, has facilitated this lucrative abuse, which continues practically unhindered at the present time. Had medical leaders exercised their natural responsibilities, this situation could have been prevented. For example, if research, seminars, and presentations had been more critically and objectively reviewed, FES's efficacy would have been proven or disproven before it was allowed to become widely marketed, adopted, and performed. A comprehensive list of surgical indications and long-term outcome studies would have reduced the number of unnecessary sinus surgeries and their complications. A substantive credentialing process would have prevented unskilled surgeons from operating. Requiring all specialists who manage sinusitis to learn how to perform comprehensive intranasal examinations would have enabled better management and follow-up. A system of physician self-policing would have meant that abusive surgeons would have been reported, and would not have been allowed to expose trainees to substandard, unethical practices. Likewise, self-policing would have prevented radiologists from describing normal and nonsignificant abnormalities seen on sinus CT scans as pathological, and prevented pathologists from reporting normal specimens as abnormal (even as they hide behind labeling these abnormalities "minor").

Instead, FES has become an out-of-control, lucrative business. Hospitals encourage abuses because of the business unnecessary surgeries bring. Direct advertising and reporting in the lay media have helped increase FES's popularity. Critical voices are suppressed or ignored. Conflicts of interest have become commonplace. As a result, we now face an epidemic of unnecessary and incomplete sinus surgeries, which have resulted in deaths and serious complications, and which have significantly contributed to the escalating cost of health care.

Chapter Nine
Solutions

In chapter 2, I outlined current reforms and reforms ideas. This chapter shall propose solutions and provide analyses of issues not addressed by current reforms and the 2010 Obama health care bill. Unless the issues discussed in this book and in this chapter are seriously addressed, it is very unlikely that reform will succeed in the long run.

The Need for New Medical Leaders

That said, the medical profession will be unable to take action at the grassroots level until its leaders change. In other words, in terms of the sequence of reform, medical leaders should lead the political charge, and doctors and patients should provide grassroots political action thereafter. This is because, in the current, deep-rooted political establishments of our democracy, the public—including doctors—simply cannot start a reform. Change has to start at the leadership levels, with efforts to later acquire grassroots support. Therefore, in this chapter I'll outline how medical leaders should be reformed or replaced before they can succeed in leading the expected reform; then I'll outline what doctors should do, politically and culturally, at the grassroots level.

First, it's an unfortunate fact that, in order for medical leaders to lead reform, they *themselves* must be reformed. The previous chapters have probably made it clear that the track record of current medical leaders is not encouraging. They have chronically failed, and should not be trusted anymore to reform the system. It is unfortunately very unlikely that medical schools and teaching hospitals, in their present forms, are capable of or even willing to lead the revolution, even with the help and cooperation of the numerous current medical organizations. The American Medical Association (AMA) could have played a major leadership role in championing reform, but it has not; its history, structure, and current conservative priorities will not allow it. In sum, in spite of their contributions, the current health care players cannot be expected to succeed in a reform that puts public interests first. Their agendas often conflict with the public's health and well-being, even though common sense and democracy dictate that the public should take priority.

Therefore, we need to replace the current medical leaders with new, committed, capable, and powerful leaders who can make a difference. We also need a new entity to oversee reform, with authority over the current health care players: a powerful, apolitical, independent organization that can make and implement the needed hard decisions, which none of the present players have done or can do. Whether appointed or elected, these new leaders must be aware of and accountable for their responsibilities toward the medical industry and the public—responsibilities that transcend bookkeeping, balancing budgets, and protecting the interests of doctors, medical schools, and hospitals. Instead, these new, top leaders should be willing and able to make unpopular decisions that serve the interests of the patients and the public in general, and should be able to fight the commercialization of medicine and the prioritization of corporations' interests over patients and public health.

To reform the medical leadership, this book advocates a solution first proposed in 2004 by authors Barlett and Steele: an independent government organization that is largely immune to politics should be created, called the U.S. Council on Health Care (USCHC).[81] Such an organization would essentially be analogous to the Federal Reserve System, and would shape health care policies much as the Federal Reserve oversees the nation's money and banking policies. The Fed is largely independent from politics, run by members appointed for fourteen years by the president with the consent of the Senate. Likewise, the USCHC would work along the same lines by taking the politics out of health care and making the much-needed decisions that the current players, including the government, have not made and that market forces have succeeded in blocking.

The leaders for this new organization would be chosen for their willingness and capability to lead, their ability to resist pressures from interest groups, and their commitment to deliver the best possible education,

81   Barlett and Steele, *Critical Condition*, 239–49.

service, and research. Their fundamental responsibilities as a part of this organization should include:

1. Making the needed unpopular decisions that the market cannot make.
2. Guaranteeing that all Americans receive a defined level of basic care.
3. Paying all costs to treat catastrophic illnesses.
4. Providing critically important drug information to consumers to balance advertising hype.
5. Reversing costly but seldom-debated health care trends, such as overdiagnosis and overtreatment.
6. Negotiating the best possible drug prices for all, something that Medicare is currently forbidden to do by law.

To successfully implement reform, the USCHC would oversee and monitor the progress of reforms, make necessary adjustments in a timely manner, work to pass needed legislation, and coordinate the work of health care activists. These additional responsibilities should entail:

1. Helping current regulatory agencies establish priorities in their work and agendas. For example, the costly legal bulletproofing that administrators are obsessed with should not remain a priority in hospitals.
2. Acting as a watchdog against unfavorable legislation and unfavorable trends. For example, the Title VII programs under the Public Health Service Act help hospitals train primary care doctors. These programs saw their budgets cut by over 50 percent in 2005. Nobody raised a red flag, in spite of the country's need for more primary care providers.
3. Determining national human resource needs (such as nursing staff shortages), and making sure that these needs are addressed.
4. Acting as a bridge between different medical specialties, coordinating their activities, and arbitrating their disputes.
5. Taking a stand on major, controversial health care issues, like stem cell research and end-of-life care. If this proves not to be possible, then the USCHC should explain the controversies to the public and organize public debates.

6. Determining research priorities and helping to distribute public resources according to these priorities.
7. Ensuring that new, worthwhile knowledge and research reaches all fields of medicine in a timely manner.
8. Controlling medical advertising and working toward legislation to penalize fraud and misinformation in advertising.
9. Providing a haven for conscientious whistle-blowers.

In terms of new legislation, these leaders should focus on three areas: they should push for new additions to the Patient's Bill of Rights, for laws against irresponsible drug advertising, and for reforms to the medical malpractice system.

First, USCHC should reform patients' rights. The current laws that cover patients' rights are not complete and not always clear. The following commonsense ideas need to be added and respected as a new Patient's Bill of Rights:

1. Insurance companies must make it possible for their patrons to find a primary care physician and a specialist within a reasonable period of time. Unreasonable waits are not acceptable, and having to wait for months reflects inadequacies in doctor availability, an issue that needs to be addressed.
2. What is covered and what is not covered needs to be made very clear when a health insurance policy is bought or sold, as when car or home insurance is bought.
3. No scheduled patient should wait for more than thirty minutes before seeing the doctor. Exceptions are acceptable in cases of emergencies, but routine or repetitive delays are not acceptable.
4. Except in the case of absence, a doctor has an obligation to see a current patient for a return visit, if necessary, within a reasonable period of time. It is the doctor's responsibility to arrange his or her schedule to make this possible.
5. The doctor or a delegate should answer nonurgent patient calls and e-mails within twenty-four hours. Urgent calls need to be promptly answered.
6. Reports of consultations, studies, and tests should be sent to the referring doctor within a reasonable period of time (not to exceed one week) after the results become available. I have had to wait for months before receiving reports on sleep studies I ordered on

patients with snoring or suspected sleep apnea. Secretarial and other administrative excuses are not valid.

7. Consent forms for surgeries and procedures need to be better explained to patients before requests are made for their signatures. Consents are not pro forma documents to be signed just before a surgery or procedure.

8. A patient has the right to know who his or her surgeon is. This is an issue to be tackled by teaching institutions, where trainees are actively involved in patient care.

9. It is the surgeon's duty to contact the family immediately after the surgery to provide information, reassurance, and to answer questions.

10. The surgeon must see the patient postoperatively at least once. Delegating this responsibility to nurses, residents, or other assistants is not a justifiable practice.

Second, the USCHC needs to advocate legislation to control irresponsible medical advertising. Drug advertising has been considered by the courts as a form of speech, protected by the First Amendment. Banning ads or putting a moratorium on them is not on the table for discussion.

So, what can be done? Since the relatively late discovery of serious risks of several popular drugs, current legislators are trying to regulate advertisements in the interest of public health. These risks have also influenced popular sentiment; the *New England Journal of Medicine* reported that a telephone survey in 2007 showed that 59 percent of respondents strongly agree that the FDA should ban ads for drugs with safety problems.[82] Legislators have come up with several suggestions in response. One idea has been to pass a law giving the FDA the power to block direct-to-consumer ads for new drugs or to review and approve ads before they are aired or published. Another proposal has been to prevent ads for new medications during the first two years of their release, to allow an opportunity for better safety surveillance. Still another idea is to hold the drug companies responsible for the content of the ads and to force them to publish and advertise new knowledge about drug safety, if and when it emerges. Another option would be to hold the FDA scientists who

---

82 Miriam Shuchman, "Drug Risks and Free Speech: Can Congressman Ban Consumer Drug Ads?" *New England Journal of Medicine* 356, no. 22 (2007): 2236–39.

knowingly hide negative information about a drug before it is released personally accountable and subject to criminal prosecution.

It is unlikely that any such legislation will see the light of day under our current system; more likely, such suggestions will be challenged and the courts will rule against them because of their possible unconstitutionality. In this particular arena, therefore, we can only hope that, if the independent, apolitical medical body I've proposed is instituted, it will be able to influence and fight misleading ads in a manner that is currently impossible.

Third, the proposed medical leadership organization should address the problem of the medical malpractice system in the U.S. Adequately discussing the malpractice system in the U.S. is beyond the scope of this book and the expertise of its author. But not to mention it at all when talking about health care reform and cost control is inexcusable.

As previously detailed in this book, the medical malpractice system is a thorn in the sides of doctors and health care institutions. It adds to costs without contributing significantly to compensating victims or reducing the incidence of medical errors. Its main beneficiaries and its fiercest protectors are the lawyers. Since 1995, legislation to address chronic malpractice problems and deficiencies has passed the House of Representatives nine times, but it has always stalled in the Senate, proving the legal profession's lobbying power and the weakness and poor organization of health care professionals.

Meanwhile, the medical malpractice insurance premiums have risen 77 percent in Massachusetts since 1998.[83] To understand the seriousness of the issue, consider this example: As a neurosurgeon, Dr. Matthew Phillips has an annual base salary of $250,000. His malpractice insurance rates jumped to more than $140,000 in 2004, an almost threefold increase from 2003.[84]

We will have to wait and see if President Obama, a lawyer himself, will start the process to reform the medical malpractice industry with as much enthusiasm as he showed when trying to reform health care in general. Regardless, one of the responsibilities of the new leaders of medicine this book proposes should be to work to reform the malpractice system at any cost.

---

83   Ralph Ranalli, "Malpractice Plan Would Limit Trials," *Boston Globe*, November 13, 2003.

84   Mark Hollmer, "Can This Doctor Be Saved?" *Boston Business Journal* 23, no. 52 (January 30–February 5, 2004).

Individualized Review and Correction

So far I've discussed legislative, political, and cultural changes that need to take place, both on the leadership and grassroots levels. But once these changes are in place, I think that leaders and practitioners alike need to set about the hard—and highly individual—tasks of preventing medical errors, abuse, and fraud. Medical errors are a very urgent, serious issue, not only because of the human losses and the immeasurable suffering, but also because of their financial impact. In 1999, the Institute of Medicine (IOM) estimated that medical errors cost the nation about $37.6 billion per year. To prevent errors, monitoring and correction must be a two-way street; the new leaders who are in place should review and handle doctors with questionable ethics and skills, and in return, doctors need a forum in which to critically evaluate not only their peers, but also their superiors and administrators.

With regard to medical errors, I doubt the wisdom of the current reform ideas. At present, a ten-year plan has been proposed that includes the creation of a national center for patient safety, a mandatory reporting system, and more FDA and hospital involvement in preventing medication errors. It stresses that professional societies must play a much more active role in implementing this system.

These recommendations are certainly comprehensive and ambitious. They look most impressive on paper, but unfortunately, they may not be practical or even feasible. They rely too heavily on correcting systems and creating new ones, boiling down to additional layers of bureaucracy, with all that this implies, including an increase in cost. The report does not appear to put enough stress on the role of individuals, on the role of teaching and supervising students and trainees, and on the role of continuing medical education. Additionally, for even the most egregious errors, the only punishment proposed or implied in the report is financial. This is not good enough; financial punishment paid by malpractice insurance companies has not so far contributed to any significant improvement in medical error rates.

Therefore, with all due respect to the report's authors and their work, I believe avoidable and repetitive mistakes made by medical practitioners deserve to be exposed as an additional step in the process of medical-error prevention. There is nothing wrong with inflicting punishment if it is appropriate. In other words, we need self-regulation of the medical community, both by leaders and by peers, in the form of an institutional, user-friendly system for doctors and administrators that works and can be monitored effectively and easily—one that holds individuals responsible, *and* targets flaws in the system itself. To go one step further, we need a system to encourage and protect whistle-blowers if self-regulation and leaders fail.

Though some may balk at the term "policing," especially those who cling to false interpretations of the Hippocratic tradition that requires doctors to help one another, internal policing by the medical profession would in fact ensure that doctors ultimately experience more individual freedom and power. Instead of penalizing all doctors with demanding rules and costly requests, only the offenders that commit mistakes or bend rules (a minority) would be targeted. In that sense, self-policing is an easier, fairer, and actually the only way to ensure quality of care and to control rising costs. Those medical administrators who object to policing because of its unpleasant nature, and those doctors who resist the idea because they insist on their "independence," are missing the point. They fail to see the rewards policing would bring: the creation of a climate to encourage free speech and transparency, especially in teaching institutions. An atmosphere of concern, responsibility, and openness would replace the irresponsible culture of see-no-evil, secrecy, and silence.

My view that self-policing is necessary is not shared by all. In 2005, the president of the Institute of Medicine (IOM) proposed that, instead of thinking of training physicians to do the right thing flawlessly, we need to think of creating systems that are incapable of allowing medical professionals to do the wrong thing.[85] In other words, the IOM considers most errors to be systems-related and not attributable to individual negligence, ignorance, or misconduct. Regulators, insurance companies, and administrators tend to favor this view as well.

At first, this idea may make sense. After all, it is certainly true that the system is at fault when mistakes are committed by overworked hospital floor nurses with multiple, competing, and urgent priorities, or when a cardiac defibrillator malfunctions. But in practice, I do not think all errors are *mostly* the fault of the system. Even if they were, no matter how perfect a system is created, human factors play a significant role and always have to be kept in mind. When an error is committed by negligence, misjudgment, or ignorance—when a sleep-deprived staff member who partied the previous night administers the wrong blood transfusion,

---

85 Harvey Fineberg, quoted in AAO-HNS, "A Note from the President," *Bulletin* 25, no. 10 (2006).

or when a poorly trained MD makes a wrong diagnosis, or when an "entrepreneurial doctor" operates unnecessarily—it is not the system that is at fault. Self-policing and punishment should make sense if we make analogies with everyday life; after all, a driver is held accountable for an accident he caused even if the car malfunctioned, and a driver under the influence is accountable even if she or he does not cause an accident or an injury. In that sense, always blaming the "system" is an oversimplification of a complex problem that has multiple roots and causes. Moreover, at its very heart, the issue of self-regulation comes down to the fact that, despite numerous uncertainties, decisions need to be made by practicing doctors. Those uncertainties cannot be completely eliminated by any system, and it is these decisions that need to be monitored and looked at critically. For that reason, proper institutional training, monitoring, rehabilitation, and punishment will always be needed for quality control.

So, what concrete form should self-regulation take? I want to emphasize that there is no "blanket" solution to my suggestions; policing measures should be tailored to different specialties in different institutions by their staffs and leaders. These need not be necessarily applicable at the state or national level.

That said, at the hospital level, I propose the creation of open forums for professional reviews in which incompetent doctors and abusers of the system can be publically held responsible. For example, suspected abusers should be asked to justify their actions in professional meetings that have a climate favorable for peer criticisms. To put this suggestion in context, let's clarify that self-policing isn't a matter of "uncovering" hard-to-spot behavior at the ground level; on the contrary, abusers are usually known by their peers, by the residents, and by the nursing staff. Self-policing is not a matter of investigation, but rather of allowing peers to speak out in a transparent environment. This climate must also be inculcated, not only through the creation of forums, but also through changing the culture of teaching hospitals.

But open peer criticism and evaluation are not enough. When criticisms have been made, chiefs of services have a duty to do the unpleasant, but necessary, policing work. Over time, this aspect of their responsibilities has almost disappeared, as their focus on income has intensified. Surgeons who perform flagrantly unnecessary procedures and clinicians who abuse expensive imaging studies, for example, are not rebuked, because of the high volume of work and income they provide institutions. So they continue in their ways, not only unhindered, but often with recognition and encouragement. Instead, leaders should take action by fining doctors, suspending their duties, and requiring those that are suspected of errors or medical malpractice to undergo education and regular monitoring. In my twenty-two years at one hospital, I only witnessed a colleague lose operating privileges once; he was no longer allowed to perform a delicate neck operation, after he almost lost the patient because of his lack of skills. Fortunately, there were surgeons available then to take over and save the patient. I have not seen any surgeon reprimanded for repeatedly performing unindicated surgeries witnessed by residents and nurses. In that hospital, there is no user-friendly way to bring the issue up for discussion. The culture is to tolerate anything that brings business to the hospital.

Medical leaders should especially focus on the following areas of abuse:

1. Unnecessary surgeries. Leaders should hold surgeons responsible, irrespective of how much business they bring to hospitals. This means that surgery indications should be audited when a suspicion arises that a procedure is performed too frequently or without sufficient justification.

2. Experimental surgeries performed without the approval of the appropriate hospital credentialing bodies. Such surgeries must be better monitored and corrected. For example, an "innovative" colleague of mine once excised the epiglottises of two patients who complained of difficulty swallowing, with the expected catastrophic results. His reasoning was that the epiglottis prevented the smooth swallowing of a pill given by a radiologist during a barium swallow study. This surgeon wrongly concluded that removing a functioning epiglottis should solve the problem. He got away with this evident malpractice, and the credentialing body, of which I was a member, did not want to be involved. He should have been punished.

3. Falsified operation notes. Operation notes need to be audited; I have often seen detailed, untruthful op notes dictated about patients who had sham sinus operations.

4. Multiple operating rooms run at the same time by one surgeon. I and my colleagues have witnessed situations in which two to three operating rooms were run at the same time by one surgeon. Doesn't this raise the risk of errors and substandard care? Of course it does. Yet it is allowed to happen.

Cost Control

So far I've outlined the steps to make systemic changes on political and social levels, and how doctors and leaders need to monitor each other to control errors and fraud. A third major concern of reform should be containing the out-of-control costs of medical care.

The need to cut and then control health care costs is vital. At present, serious institutional cost-containment policies are virtually nonexistent. Volumes of laws, rules, and regulations dictated by third parties and regulators are not enough and have not worked. Doctors and hospitals have proven that they can get around regulations they do not like and outsmart the system to successfully beef up their incomes and effectively neutralize cost-cutting efforts.

Legislation, necessary to contain the costs of insurance coverage, medications, and malpractice insurance, is not the only answer. For cost-control measures to be effective in the daily practice and delivery of health care, they have to originate from within and be adopted by the medical profession and its new leaders. The cooperation, willingness, and commitment of the medical profession are mandatory; professionals can and should independently adopt effective cost-cutting measures and drop the prevalent attitude that medicine is a business. As with policing measures, cost-containment policies need to be worked out by each institution, applicable to its medical and administrative staff. These should be capable of easy, regular monitoring, and should be modified when the need arises. The new leaders this book advocates putting in place should be able to accomplish this task.

Conclusion

In conclusion, this book is unique in the current debates about health care reform in that it attracts attention to ignored issues that absolutely need to be resolved for reform to succeed. It stresses the fact that without the involvement and commitment of the medical profession, no reform can be effective and lasting. The laws, regulations, and discussions currently under way are not enough for an effective reform. Competition, as a quality ensurer, has badly failed in health care. Why be stubborn and keep expecting success from it? To be eligible and capable of leading reform, the medical profession needs to reform itself first with the help of the new leadership proposed in this book. There is a need for serious accountability at all levels.

All of this will require no less than a revolution in health care. In democracies, the term "revolution" is usually avoided due to unpopular connotations. A chief of service I know often repeated the mantra that change or improvement should be accomplished "by evolution and not revolution"; hence, his were slow to arrive. This was a matter of principle to him, and it should not be imposed on everyone. Revolutions seem to be associated in the public's mind with dictatorships in the third world and carry negative and risky implications. But revolutions can be good. The American revolution of 1775 and the French revolution of 1789 were costly but good revolutions. So, the idea of a revolution should not to be rejected on principle's sake, even in our democracy. Revolutionary changes are the only solution to the health care crisis, and should be started and then led by a new, rehabilitated, and reoriented medical profession and its new leadership.

Just as revolution should be embraced and not avoided, the solutions proposed in this book should not be labeled as simplistic, impractical, or unattainable and therefore discarded a priori. There are no easy or fast solutions on the table, and much of the hard work needs to be done by the medical profession. But change has to happen—it's not a matter of dreams, but rather a matter of grand vision that's absolutely necessary. Was President Kennedy merely a dreamer when he promised the voyage to the moon? Were the imaginative investigators who initiated organ transplants, in vitro fertilization, gene therapy, and other remarkable advances in medicine chasing rainbows? The solutions the book proposes are not easy to design and apply, but they are necessary and unavoidable. And they're far more realistic than waiting for the impossible to happen: for the insurance and pharmaceutical companies to become philanthropic; for the legislators to become insensitive to their generous corporate contributors; for the administrators to alter their priorities; and for the lawyers to become saints. We do not have to wait for the impossible; we need to take action now, before the system collapses and the health care reform signed into law in 2010 fails to achieve all its intended long-term purposes.

About the Author

Dr. Salman studied and trained at the American University of Beirut and at the Johns Hopkins Medical Institutions. He spent his professional life in academic medicine. He is a former Professor & Chairman of the Department of Otolaryngology at his Alma Mater. In 2009 and after 23 years, he retired from being a Surgeon and Director of the Sinus Center at the Massachusetts Eye & Ear Infirmary, and a lecturer at Harvard Medical School in Boston, Massachusetts. He has published 53 papers in scientific journals and authored chapters in medical textbooks. He served as Guest Editor and as Section Editor in Medical Journals. He also authored 2 textbooks, "An Atlas of the Nasopharynx" and "An Atlas of Diagnostic Nasal Endoscopy".

He served as a Visiting Professor in several medical schools. He is a member of the Alpha Omega Alpha Honor Medical Society, and received many awards including the prestigious Penrose Award for the Faculties of Medical Sciences, on graduation from the American University of Beirut.

In 1972, he was the Lebanese Minister of Public Health. During the Lebanese war, he also served as Minister of the Interior, and minister of Housing and Cooperatives, from 1976 to 1979.

He helped introduce to Lebanon the International Work Camps for Conscientious Objectors.